Best Cookie Book Ever!

by Debbi Fields
and the Editors of Time-Life Books

TIME
LIFE
BOOKS

Time-Life Books, Alexandria, Virginia

Contents

Simple but versatile, drop cookies are the classic after-school snack: Mix up the ingredients in a bowl, drop dough by spoonfuls onto a cookie sheet, and watch them spread out into yummy fresh treats as they bake. There's a cookie for every taste here, including Carrot Fruit Jumbles, Monster Chunk, and every possible variation on the perennial favorite, Chocolate Chip.

When you feel like baking something a little different, choose one of Mrs. Fields' filled cookie recipes. Folding rich dough around nuts, jellies, or fruits produces festive cookies that are well worth the extra bit of time they take. And for that perfect gift, you can't beat a decorated tin packed with Glazed Honey-Nut Rolls, Pineapple Pocket Pies, or traditional Linzer Cookies.

Fancy Cookies

Here are dressed-up cookies to delight everyone in the family. The children will love rolling out sugar-cookie dough, cutting out fun shapes, and decorating the finished goodies with icing, candies, and sprinkles. And for sophisticated grownup tastes—perhaps at an afternoon tea or a dessert party—try Almond Crunch Cookies, Russian Tea Cakes, or Double-Dipped Chocolate Shortbread Cookies.

Bar Cookies. . . . .

When you're pressed for time, bar cookies are ideal: Just mix the batter, spread it in a pan, and bake. Recipes in this section range from the elegant Triple-Layered Lemon Bars to child-pleasing Peanut Butter & Jelly Squares and Mother Lode Brownies. Bar cookies are perfect for packing in a lunchbox or picnic basket, and they also freeze well, to provide an instant snack on a future day.

Special Treats . . . .

Nothing marks a special occasion better than a truly special dessert from your kitchen, and these pies, tarts, cakes, and other sweets all bear the Mrs. Fields stamp of memorable flavor. Try Mocha Mousse Cheesecake for a Father's Day cookout, Raspberry and White Chocolate Tart for a bridal shower, or Sweetie Pie Cookie Dough Ice Cream to complete an anniversary dinner.

Introduction

Are any treats more universally loved than homemade cookies, warm out of the oven?

At a time when convenience foods are more popular than ever, homemade cookies and other desserts are staging a major comeback. Taste no doubt has a lot to do with that, but perhaps it's also because home-baked goods tell your family and friends that you care enough to take the time to make it yourself.

No one knows this better than Debbi Fields, mother of five and surely the most celebrated cookie-baker of all time. Although her recipes today are loved the world over, they actually began right at home, in her own kitchen, with her family as taste-testers. It didn't take long for "rich" and "delicious" to become synonymous with "Mrs. Fields."

Now, to help you create these premium baked treats in your own home, we've collected the best of the best—a roundup of favorite recipes from the kitchen of Debbi Fields, including some new ones never before published.

With 130 mouth-watering selections, *Mrs. Fields Best Cookie Book Ever!* may well become your dessert "bible," the only cookbook you'll ever need to whip up the perfect sweets for any occasion. Here are recipes for every type of cookie imaginable, from classics like Blue-Ribbon Chocolate Chip Cookies and Oatmeal Raisin Chews to more exotic cookies such as Maple Pecan Butter Balls and Macadamia Nut Coconut Crisps. You'll also find recipes for those special times when you need a dressier dessert—elegant crowd-pleasers like Milk Chocolate Toffee Cream Pie or Lemon Custard Cake.

Armed with all these choices, you'll surely be able to satisfy every sweet tooth in your life, and touch a lot of hearts with your thoughtfulness.

Drop Cookies

Blue-Ribbon Chocolate Chip Cookies

2½ cups all-purpose flour
½ teaspoon baking soda
¼ teaspoon salt
1 cup (packed) dark brown sugar
½ cup granulated sugar
2 sticks (1 cup) salted butter, softened

2 large eggs
2 teaspoons vanilla extract
12 ounces semisweet chocolate chips
(about 2 cups)

Yield: About 3½ dozen

- Preheat oven to 300°F.
- In medium bowl, combine flour, soda, and salt. Mix well with wire whisk. Set aside.
- In a large bowl with an electric mixer, blend sugars at medium speed. Add butter and mix to form a grainy paste, scraping down the sides of the bowl. Add eggs and vanilla extract, and mix at medium speed until just blended. Do not overmix.
- Add the flour mixture and chocolate chips, and blend at low speed until just mixed. Do not overmix.
- Drop the dough by rounded tablespoons onto an ungreased cookie sheet, 2 inches apart. Bake for 18 to 22 minutes or until golden brown. Transfer cookies immediately to a cool surface with a spatula.

Drop each heaping tablespoon of dough onto the cookie sheet, taking care to leave about 2 inches between each cookie. As they bake, the cookies will spread.

Apple Oatmeal Cookies

COOKIES
2½ cups all-purpose flour
1 cup quick oats (not instant)
½ teaspoon salt
1 teaspoon baking soda
1 teaspoon ground cinnamon
¼ teaspoon ground cloves
2 teaspoons grated lemon zest
(1 medium lemon)
1 cup (packed) dark brown sugar
1½ sticks (¾ cup) salted butter, softened

1 large egg
½ cup unsweetened applesauce
½ cup honey
1 cup fresh apple, peeled and finely
chopped (1 medium apple)
6 ounces raisins (about 1 cup)

TOPPING
½ cup quick oats

Yield: About 4 dozen

- Preheat oven to 300°F.
- In medium bowl combine flour, oats, salt, soda, cinnamon, cloves, and lemon zest. Mix well with a wire whisk. Set aside.
- Cream sugar and butter together in a large bowl using an electric mixer. Add egg, applesauce, and honey and beat at medium speed until smooth.
- Add the flour mixture, fresh apple, and raisins, and blend at low speed until just combined. Do not overmix. Dough will be quite soft.
- Drop by rounded tablespoons onto ungreased baking sheets, 1½ inches apart. If you wish, sprinkle the cookies with oats. Bake for 18 to 22 minutes or until bottoms are golden.

Pumpkin Harvest Cookies

2¼ cups all-purpose flour
1 teaspoon pumpkin pie spice
½ teaspoon baking soda
2 sticks (1 cup) unsalted butter
1½ cups (packed) dark brown sugar
1 cup solid-packed unsweetened pumpkin
purée

2 large eggs
1 tablespoon vanilla extract
10 ounces white chocolate, coarsely
chopped
1 cup pecan halves and pieces, toasted

Yield: About 3 dozen

- Preheat the oven to 300°F.
- In a small bowl, combine the flour, pumpkin pie spice, and baking soda.
- In a medium bowl with an electric mixer, cream the butter and sugar. Beat in the pumpkin purée. Beat in the eggs and vanilla. Beat in the flour mixture until just combined. Stir in the white chocolate and pecans.
- Drop the dough by rounded tablespoons 2 inches apart on an ungreased cookie sheet. Bake for 20 to 22 minutes, or until just set. Transfer to wire racks to cool.

8

Chocolate Chip Dough to Go

2 cups all-purpose flour
1 cup quick oats
½ teaspoon baking powder
¼ teaspoon salt
2 sticks (1 cup) unsalted butter, softened
¾ cup (packed) light brown sugar
¾ cup granulated sugar

2 large eggs
2 teaspoons vanilla extract
1 cup coarsely chopped pecans
12 ounces semisweet chocolate chips
(about 2 cups)

Yield: About 4 dozen

- In a medium bowl, combine the flour, oats, baking powder, and salt. In another medium bowl with an electric mixer, cream the butter and sugars. Beat in the eggs and vanilla. Gently beat in the flour mixture; then stir in the pecans and chocolate chips.
- Turn half of the dough out onto a sheet of wax paper. Shape into a log 2 inches in diameter. Roll up the log of dough in the wax paper and twist the ends closed. Repeat with the remaining dough. Chill until firm. The cookie dough can be refrigerated for 1 week or frozen for 6 months stored in an airtight plastic bag.
- To bake the cookies, preheat the oven to 300°F. If using frozen dough, let it soften slightly at room temperature, then cut the dough log into ½-inch-thick slices. Place the slices on an ungreased cookie sheet 2 inches apart. Bake for 22 to 24 minutes, or until set.

Cut the chilled dough into ½-inch thick slices and place 2 inches apart on an ungreased cookie sheet.

Malted Milk Cookies

2½ cups all-purpose flour
¾ cup plain malted milk powder
½ teaspoon baking soda
¼ teaspoon salt
1 cup granulated sugar
½ cup (packed) light brown sugar
2 sticks (1 cup) salted butter, softened

2 large eggs
2 teaspoons vanilla extract
2 tablespoons sweetened condensed milk
12 ounces milk chocolate chips
(about 2 cups)

Yield: About 3½ dozen

- Preheat oven to 300°F.
- In medium bowl, combine flour, malted milk powder, soda, and salt. Mix well with a wire whisk. Set aside.
- Blend sugars using an electric mixer set at medium speed. Add butter and mix, occasionally scraping down the sides of the bowl. Add the eggs, vanilla, and condensed milk, and beat at medium speed until light and fluffy.

- Add the flour mixture and chocolate chips, and blend at low speed until just combined. Do not overmix.
- Drop by rounded tablespoons onto ungreased cookie sheets, 2 inches apart. Bake 22 to 25 minutes until cookies are slightly brown along edges. Transfer cookies immediately to cool surface with a spatula.

Carrot Fruit Jumbles

2½ cups all-purpose flour
1 teaspoon baking soda
½ teaspoon baking powder
½ teaspoon ground cloves
2 teaspoons ground cinnamon
¼ teaspoon salt
1 cup quick oats (not instant)
¾ cup (packed) dark brown sugar
¾ cup granulated sugar

2 sticks (1 cup) salted butter, softened
2 large eggs
2 teaspoons vanilla extract
2 cups grated carrot
(2 or 3 medium carrots)
½ cup crushed pineapple, drained
4 ounces chopped walnuts (about 1 cup)

Yield: About 4 dozen

- Preheat oven to 350°F.
- In a medium bowl combine flour, soda, baking powder, cloves, cinnamon, salt, and oats. Mix well with a wire whisk and set aside.
- In a large bowl with an electric mixer, blend sugars. Add butter and mix to form a grainy paste. Scrape down sides of bowl.
- Add eggs and vanilla, and beat at medium speed until light and fluffy. Add carrots, pineapple, and nuts, and blend until combined. Batter will appear lumpy.
- Add flour mixture and blend at low speed until just combined. Do not overmix.
- Drop by rounded teaspoons onto ungreased baking sheets, 1½ inches apart. Bake 13 to 15 minutes, taking care not to brown cookies. Immediately transfer cookies with a spatula to a cool, flat surface.

Kids Bake 'Em Cookies

$1\frac{1}{4}$ *cups all-purpose flour*
$\frac{1}{2}$ *teaspoon baking soda*
$\frac{1}{8}$ *teaspoon salt*
1 stick ($\frac{1}{2}$ cup) salted butter, softened
$\frac{1}{4}$ *cup granulated sugar*

$\frac{1}{2}$ *cup honey*
6 ounces semisweet chocolate chips
(about 1 cup)

Yield: About 2 dozen

- Preheat oven 300°F.
- In a small bowl combine flour, soda, and salt. Mix well with a wire whisk and set aside.
- In a medium bowl, blend butter, sugar, and honey with an electric mixer at medium speed. Beat until light and soft, then scrape sides of bowl.
- Add the flour mixture and chocolate chips, and blend at low speed just until combined. Do not overmix.
- Drop dough by rounded teaspoons onto ungreased cookie sheets, $1\frac{1}{2}$ inches apart. Bake 18 to 20 minutes or until light golden brown. Immediately transfer cookies with a spatula to a cool, flat surface.

Pecan Supremes

2 cups all-purpose flour
½ teaspoon baking soda
¼ teaspoon salt
¾ cup quick oats
¾ cup (packed) dark brown sugar
¾ cup granulated sugar
2 sticks (1 cup) salted butter, softened

2 large eggs
2 teaspoons vanilla extract
4 ounces chopped pecans (about 1 cup)
6 ounces semisweet chocolate chips
(about 1 cup)

Yield: About 3 dozen

- Preheat oven to 300°F.
- In a medium bowl combine flour, soda, salt, and oats. Mix well with wire whisk and set aside.
- In a large bowl, blend sugars with an electric mixer at medium speed. Add butter and mix to form a grainy paste. Scrape down sides of bowl, then add eggs and vanilla. Beat at medium speed until light and fluffy.
- Add the flour mixture, pecans, and chocolate chips, and blend at low speed just until combined. Do not overmix.
- Drop dough by rounded tablespoons onto ungreased cookie sheets, 1½ inches apart. Bake for 18 to 20 minutes. Immediately transfer cookies with a spatula to a cool, flat surface.

Double-Chocolate Peanut Butter Cookies

6 ounces semisweet chocolate, coarsely
chopped
2 cups all-purpose flour
$\frac{1}{2}$ teaspoon baking soda
$\frac{1}{4}$ teaspoon salt
$\frac{3}{4}$ cup (packed) dark brown sugar
$\frac{3}{4}$ cup granulated sugar
2 sticks (1 cup) unsalted butter, softened

1 cup creamy peanut butter
2 large eggs
2 teaspoons vanilla extract
12 ounces milk chocolate chips
(about 2 cups)
24 to 30 whole shelled peanuts

Yield: About 2 dozen

- Preheat the oven to 300°F. In a double boiler, melt the semisweet chocolate over hot, not simmering, water. Set aside to cool to about room temperature.
- In a small bowl, combine the flour, baking soda, and salt.
- In a medium bowl, combine the brown and granulated sugars, then add the butter and beat until well combined. Add the peanut butter and beat until smooth. Add the eggs and vanilla, and beat until just combined. Add the flour mixture and the milk chocolate chips, and beat until no streaks of flour are visible.

- Pour in the melted chocolate and mix partially with a wooden spoon until marbleized. Drop the dough in 3-tablespoon mounds 2 inches apart on an ungreased baking sheet. Top each with one whole peanut. Bake for 23 minutes, or until just set but still soft. Cool on the cookie sheet for 30 seconds, then transfer to wire racks to cool completely.

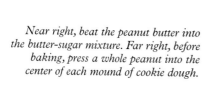

Near right, beat the peanut butter into the butter-sugar mixture. Far right, before baking, press a whole peanut into the center of each mound of cookie dough.

White Chocolate Cookies with Chocolate Chunks

2 sticks (1 cup) unsalted butter, softened
2½ cups all-purpose flour
1 teaspoon baking soda
¼ teaspoon salt
3 ounces white chocolate, finely chopped
½ cup granulated sugar
½ cup (packed) light brown sugar

2 large eggs, at room temperature
2 teaspoons vanilla extract
8 ounces semisweet chocolate, cut into chunks

Yield: About 3 dozen

- Preheat the oven to 300°F. Cut 4 tablespoons of the butter into ¼-inch cubes.
- In a small bowl, combine the flour, baking soda, and salt.
- In a double boiler, melt the white chocolate with the butter, stirring until melted and smooth, about 10 minutes. Set aside to cool slightly.
- In a large bowl with an electric mixer, cream the remaining 1½ sticks of butter with the granulated and brown sugars. Beat in the eggs one at a time, beating well after each addition. Beat in the white chocolate mixture and vanilla. On low speed, gradually beat in the flour mixture until just combined. Stir in the semisweet chocolate chunks.
- Drop the dough by rounded tablespoons 2 inches apart onto an ungreased cookie sheet. Bake for about 20 minutes, or until the edges of the cookies begin to brown lightly (the cookies will still be soft in the center). Cool on the cookie sheet for 1 minute, then transfer to wire racks to cool completely.

Mocha Chunk Cookies

2½ cups all-purpose flour
⅓ cup unsweetened cocoa powder
½ teaspoon baking soda
¼ teaspoon salt
2 teaspoons instant coffee crystals
(French roast or other dark coffee)
2 teaspoons coffee liqueur
1 cup granulated sugar

¾ cup (packed) dark brown sugar
2 sticks (1 cup) salted butter, softened
2 large eggs
10 ounces semisweet chocolate bar,
coarsely chopped (about 2 cups)

Yield: About 4 dozen

- Preheat oven to 300°F.
- In a medium bowl, combine flour, cocoa, soda, and salt. Mix well with a wire whisk and set aside.
- In a small bowl, dissolve coffee crystals in coffee liqueur and set aside.
- In a large bowl, blend sugars with an electric mixer at medium speed. Add butter and mix to form a grainy paste. Scrape down sides of bowl.

Then add eggs and dissolved coffee crystals, and beat at medium speed until smooth.
- Add the flour mixture and chocolate chunks, and blend at low speed just until combined. Do not overmix.
- Drop by rounded tablespoons onto ungreased cookie sheet, 2 inches apart. Bake for 20 to 22 minutes. Immediately transfer cookies with a spatula to a cool, flat surface.

16

Banana Nut Cookies

2⅔ cups all-purpose flour
½ teaspoon baking soda
¼ teaspoon salt
1 cup (packed) light brown sugar
½ cup granulated sugar
2 sticks (1 cup) salted butter, softened
1 large egg
1 teaspoon crème de banana liqueur or banana extract

¾ cup mashed ripe banana
(1 medium banana)
12 ounces semisweet chocolate chips
(about 2 cups)
4 ounces chopped walnuts (about 1 cup)

Yield: About 4 dozen

- Preheat oven to 300°F.
- In medium bowl, combine flour, soda, and salt. Mix well with a wire whisk. Set aside.
- In large bowl with an electric mixer blend sugars at medium speed. Add butter and mix to form a grainy paste, scraping down the sides of the bowl. Add egg, liqueur, and banana, and beat at medium speed until smooth.
- Add the flour mixture, 1 cup of the chocolate chips, and the walnuts, and blend at low speed until just combined. Do not overmix.
- Drop by rounded tablespoons onto ungreased cookie sheets, 2 inches apart. Sprinkle cookies with chocolate chips, 6 to 8 per cookie. Bake 20 to 24 minutes or until cookie edges begin to brown. Transfer immediately to a cool surface with a spatula.

Chocolate Mint Cookies

2²/₃ cups all-purpose flour
½ teaspoon baking soda
¼ teaspoon salt
½ cup unsweetened cocoa powder
¾ cup (packed) light brown sugar
²/₃ cup granulated sugar
2 sticks (1 cup) salted butter, softened

3 large eggs
1 teaspoon mint extract
10 ounces mint chocolate chips
(about 1¾ cups)

Yield: About 3 dozen

- Preheat oven to 300°F.
- In a medium bowl, combine flour, soda, salt, and cocoa powder. Mix well with a wire whisk and set aside.
- In a large bowl, blend sugars with an electric mixer at medium speed. Add butter and beat to form a grainy paste. Scrape sides of bowl, then add eggs and mint extract. Beat at medium speed until light and fluffy.
- Add the flour mixture and chocolate chips, and blend at low speed just until combined. Do not overmix.
- Drop dough by rounded tablespoons onto ungreased cookie sheets, 1½ inches apart. Bake for 19 to 21 minutes. Immediately transfer cookies with a spatula to a cool, flat surface.

Lemon Chocolate Chip Buttons

2 cups all-purpose flour
½ teaspoon baking soda
1 teaspoon ground coriander
1½ sticks (¾ cup) salted butter, softened
1 cup granulated sugar
2 large eggs

1½ teaspoons lemon extract
9 ounces mini chocolate chips
(about 1½ cups)

Yield: About 4 dozen

- Preheat oven to 300°F.
- In a medium bowl combine flour, soda, and coriander with a wire whisk. Set aside.
- In a large bowl cream butter and sugar with an electric mixer at medium speed to form a grainy paste. Add eggs and lemon extract, and beat well. Scrape down sides of bowl.
- Add the flour mixture and the chocolate chips, and blend at low speed just until combined. Do not overmix.
- Drop dough by teaspoons onto ungreased baking sheets, 1½ inches apart. Bake for 14 to 15 minutes on center rack of oven. Do not brown. Immediately transfer cookies with a spatula to a cool, flat surface.

Peanut Butter Oatmeal Ranch Cookies

¾ cup whole-wheat flour
¾ cup all-purpose flour
½ teaspoon baking powder
1 cup oats (old fashioned or quick)
1 cup (packed) light brown sugar
1 stick (½ cup) salted butter, softened
½ cup creamy peanut butter

¼ cup honey
2 large eggs
2 teaspoons vanilla extract
6 ounces raisins (about 1 cup)
3 ounces sunflower seeds (about ½ cup)

Yield: About 3 dozen

- Preheat oven to 300°F.
- In a medium bowl, combine flours, baking powder, and oats. Mix well with a wire whisk and set aside.
- In a large bowl, beat sugar and butter with an electric mixer at medium speed to form a grainy paste. Blend together the peanut butter, honey, eggs, and vanilla. Scrape down sides of bowl.
- Add the flour mixture, raisins, and sunflower seeds. Blend at low speed just until combined. Do not overmix.
- Drop by rounded tablespoons onto ungreased baking sheets, 2 inches apart. Bake for 18 to 22 minutes until bottoms turn golden brown. Immediately transfer cookies with a spatula to a cool, flat surface.

Cashew and Coconut Cookies

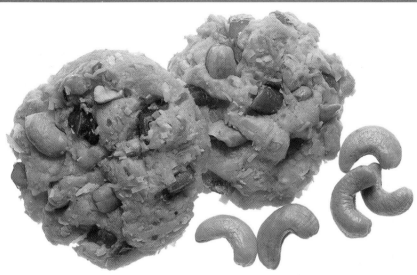

2¼ cups all-purpose flour
½ teaspoon baking soda
¼ teaspoon salt
¾ cup (packed) light brown sugar
½ cup granulated sugar
1½ sticks (¾ cup) salted butter, softened
2 large eggs
2 teaspoons vanilla extract

½ cup sweetened shredded coconut
4 ounces chopped, unsalted raw
cashews (about 1 cup)
4 ounces chopped dates (about 1 cup)
2 ounces sweetened shredded coconut
(about ¼ cup), reserved for topping

Yield: About 2½ dozen

- Preheat oven to 300°F.
- In a medium bowl, combine flour, soda, and salt. Mix well with a wire whisk and set aside.
- In a medium bowl, combine sugars with an electric mixer at medium speed. Add butter and mix to form a grainy paste. Add eggs and vanilla, and beat until smooth.
- Add flour mixture, coconut, cashews, and dates. Blend at low speed just until combined. Do not overmix.

- Drop by rounded tablespoons onto ungreased baking sheets, 2 inches apart. Sprinkle tops lightly with reserved coconut.
- Bake for 18 to 22 minutes or until bottoms turn golden brown. With a spatula, transfer cookies to a cool, flat surface.

Sprinkle about a teaspoon of coconut on top of each cookie before sliding the sheets into the oven. When the cookies have finished baking, the coconut will take on a golden, toasted color.

Fruitcake Cookies

2 cups all-purpose flour
$\frac{1}{2}$ teaspoon baking powder
1 cup quick oats (not instant)
2 sticks (1 cup) salted butter, softened
$1\frac{1}{2}$ cups (packed) light brown sugar
$\frac{1}{4}$ cup unsulfurized molasses
2 teaspoons brandy
2 teaspoons vanilla extract
2 teaspoons almond extract

2 large eggs
3 ounces raisins (about $\frac{1}{2}$ cup)
4 ounces chopped pecans (about 1 cup)
2 ounces chopped almonds (about $\frac{1}{2}$ cup)
$13\frac{1}{2}$ ounces candied cherries, chopped
(about 2 cups)

Yield: About $4\frac{1}{2}$ dozen

- Preheat oven to 300°F.
- In a medium bowl, combine flour, baking powder, and oats. Mix well with a wire whisk and set aside.
- In a large bowl, cream butter and sugar with an electric mixer at medium speed. Mix to form a grainy paste. Add molasses, brandy, almond and vanilla extracts and eggs; beat until smooth.
- Add flour mixture, raisins, pecans, almonds, and cherries. Blend at low speed just until combined. Do not overmix.

- Drop by rounded tablespoons onto ungreased baking sheets, $1\frac{1}{2}$ inches apart. Bake for 22 to 24 minutes or until cookies are set.
- Let cookies set on pan for a few minutes, then transfer to a cool, flat surface. Top each cookie with a candied cherry half.

These cookies are fruitcake made easy. You just blend everything in your mixer—first the dry ingredients, then the wet, and finally the fruit pieces. Both a hand mixer or a stand-up mixer work fine.

Chocolate Chip Raisin Cookies

2 cups all-purpose flour
½ teaspoon baking powder
⅓ cup (packed) light brown sugar
1 cup granulated sugar
2 sticks (1 cup) salted butter, softened
2 large eggs

2 teaspoons vanilla extract
12 ounces raisins (about 2 cups)
12 ounces semisweet chocolate chips
(about 2 cups)

Yield: About 4½ dozen

- Preheat oven to 300°F.
- In medium bowl, combine flour and baking powder. Mix well with wire whisk. Set aside.
- Blend sugars in a large bowl using an electric mixer set at medium speed. Add butter and mix until grainy, scraping down the sides of the bowl. Add eggs and vanilla extract, and mix at medium speed until smooth.

- Add the flour mixture, raisins, and chocolate chips. Blend at low speed until just combined. Do not overmix.
- Drop by rounded tablespoons onto ungreased baking sheets, 1½ inches apart. Bake 18 to 20 minutes. Transfer cookies immediately to a cool, flat surface using a spatula.

Orange Chocolate Chunk Cookies

2½ cups all-purpose flour
½ teaspoon baking soda
¼ teaspoon salt
1 teaspoon grated orange peel
(1 medium orange)
1 cup granulated sugar
½ cup (packed) light brown sugar

2 sticks (1 cup) salted butter, softened
2 large eggs
1 teaspoon orange extract
8 ounces semisweet chocolate bar, coarsely
chopped (about 1½ cups)

Yield: About 2½ dozen

- Preheat oven to 300°F.
- In a medium bowl, combine flour, soda, salt, and orange peel. Mix well with a wire whisk and set aside.
- In a large bowl, blend sugars with an electric mixer at medium speed. Add butter and beat to form a grainy paste, scraping sides of bowl if needed. Add eggs and orange extract, and beat at medium speed until light and fluffy.

- Add the flour mixture and chopped chocolate. Blend at low speed just until combined. Do not overmix.
- Drop by rounded tablespoons onto ungreased cookie sheets, 1½ inches apart. Bake for 18 to 22 minutes until cookies are slightly brown along edges. Transfer cookies immediately to a cool surface with a spatula.

Eggnog Cookies

2¼ cups all-purpose flour
1 teaspoon baking powder
½ teaspoon ground cinnamon
½ teaspoon ground nutmeg
1¼ cups granulated sugar
1½ sticks (¾ cup) salted butter, softened

½ cup eggnog
1 teaspoon vanilla extract
2 large egg yolks
1 tablespoon ground nutmeg

Yield: About 3 dozen

- Preheat oven to 300°F.
- In a medium bowl, combine flour, baking powder, cinnamon, and nutmeg. Mix well with a wire whisk and set aside.
- In a large bowl, cream sugar and butter with an electric mixer to form a grainy paste. Add eggnog, vanilla, and egg yolks and beat at medium speed until smooth.
- Add the flour mixture and beat at low speed just until combined. Do not overmix.
- Drop by rounded teaspoons onto ungreased baking sheets, 1 inch apart. Sprinkle lightly with nutmeg. Bake for 23 to 25 minutes or until bottoms turn light brown. Transfer to cool, flat surface immediately with a spatula.

Black-and-Whites

$2\frac{1}{4}$ cups all-purpose flour
$\frac{1}{2}$ cup unsweetened cocoa powder
$\frac{1}{2}$ teaspoon baking soda
$\frac{1}{4}$ teaspoon salt
1 cup (packed) dark brown sugar
$\frac{3}{4}$ cup granulated sugar
2 sticks (1 cup) salted butter, softened
3 large eggs

2 teaspoons vanilla extract
$5\frac{1}{4}$ ounces semisweet chocolate bar,
coarsely chopped (about 1 cup)
$5\frac{1}{4}$ ounces white chocolate bar, coarsely
chopped (about 1 cup)

Yield: About 3 dozen

- Preheat oven to 300°F.
- In medium bowl, combine flour, cocoa, soda, and salt. Mix well with a wire whisk. Set aside.
- Blend sugars in a large bowl using an electric mixer set at medium speed. Add butter and mix to form a grainy paste, scraping down the sides of the bowl. Add eggs and vanilla, and beat at medium speed until smooth.

- Add the flour mixture and chocolates, and blend at low speed until just combined. Do not overmix.
- Drop by rounded tablespoons onto ungreased cookie sheets, 2 inches apart. Bake 18 to 22 minutes. Transfer cookies immediately to a cool, flat surface.

Marbles

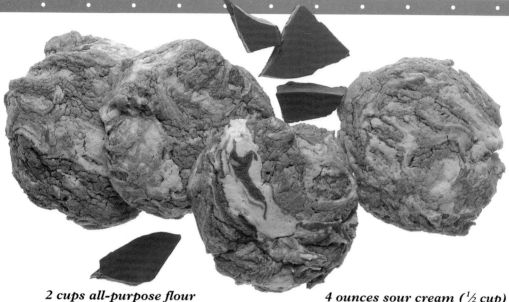

2 cups all-purpose flour
½ teaspoon baking powder
¼ teaspoon salt
½ cup (packed) light brown sugar
½ cup granulated sugar
1 stick (½ cup) salted butter, softened
1 large egg

4 ounces sour cream (½ cup)
1 teaspoon vanilla extract
6 ounces semisweet chocolate chips
(about 1 cup)

Yield: About 2½ dozen

- Preheat oven to 300°F.
- In medium bowl, combine flour, baking powder, and salt with wire whisk. Set aside.
- Combine sugars in a large bowl using an electric mixer set at medium speed. Add butter and beat until batter is grainy. Add egg, sour cream, and vanilla, and beat at medium speed until light and fluffy. Scrape bowl. Add the flour mixture and blend at low speed until just combined. Do not overmix.

- Place chocolate chips in double boiler over hot, but not boiling, water. Stir constantly until melted. Or, place chips in a microwave-proof bowl and microwave on high, stirring every 20 seconds until melted.
- Cool chocolate for a few minutes and pour over cookie batter. Using a wooden spoon or rubber spatula, lightly fold melted chocolate into the dough. Do not mix chocolate completely into cookie dough.
- Drop by rounded tablespoons, 2 inches apart, onto ungreased cookie sheets. Bake 20 to 22 minutes. Do not brown. Quickly transfer cookies to a cool surface.

Fold the cool melted chocolate into the cookie batter, stirring lightly with a wooden spoon (far left). Continue stirring only until the chocolate is well distributed and creates a swirled, marbleized pattern (left).

Low-Fat Chocolate Cookies

2⅔ *cups all-purpose flour*
½ *cup unsweetened cocoa powder*
1 *teaspoon baking soda*
½ *teaspoon salt*
¾ *cup (packed) dark brown sugar*
¾ *cup granulated sugar*
⅓ *cup canola oil*

½ *cup unsweetened applesauce*
3 *egg whites*
2 *teaspoons vanilla extract*
½ *cup mini semisweet chocolate chips*

Yield: About 5½ dozen

- In a medium bowl, combine the flour, cocoa, baking soda, and salt.
- In another medium bowl with an electric mixer, blend the brown and granulated sugars. Slowly beat in the oil. Beat in the applesauce, egg whites, and vanilla, and blend on low speed until smooth.
- Add the flour mixture and blend on low speed until the dough is just combined. Refrigerate the dough until firm, about 1 hour.

- Preheat the oven to 300°F.
- Roll the dough into small (1-inch) balls, place on a cookie sheet and flatten slightly. Sprinkle with the mini chocolate chips, then bake for 17 to 19 minutes (do not overbake; when the cookies cool they will get hard). Transfer the cookies to wire racks to cool.

Chocolate Cashew Crunch

4 tablespoons (1/4 cup) unsalted butter
1/3 cup (packed) light brown sugar
1/4 cup light corn syrup
1/2 cup finely chopped salted cashews
1/3 cup all-purpose flour

1 1/2 teaspoons vanilla extract
6 ounces milk chocolate chips
(about 1 cup)

Yield: About 3 dozen

- Preheat the oven to 350°F. Butter and flour a cookie sheet.
- In a small saucepan, melt the butter over medium heat. Add the brown sugar and corn syrup, then bring to a boil over medium heat, stirring constantly, until the sugar dissolves, 3 to 5 minutes. Remove from the heat.
- Stir in the cashews, flour, and vanilla. Drop the batter in 1/2-teaspoon mounds 2 inches apart onto the prepared cookie sheet. Using a small spatula, spread each mound into a circle.

- Bake for 8 to 10 minutes, or until browned, rotating the pan back to front after 4 minutes. Cool on the cookie sheet for about 30 seconds, then transfer to wire racks to cool completely.
- In a small bowl set over a small saucepan, melt the chocolate over hot, not simmering, water. Dip the cookies halfway into the chocolate and return to the racks to set.

Double-Rich Chocolate Cookies

2½ cups all-purpose flour
½ teaspoon baking soda
¼ teaspoon salt
½ cup unsweetened cocoa powder
1 cup (packed) dark brown sugar
¾ cup granulated sugar
2 sticks (1 cup) salted butter, softened

3 large eggs
2 teaspoons vanilla extract
12 ounces semisweet chocolate chips
(about 2 cups)

Yield: About 4 dozen

- Preheat oven 300°F.
- In a medium bowl, combine flour, soda, salt, and cocoa powder. Mix well with a wire whisk and set aside.
- In a large bowl, blend sugars with an electric mixer at medium speed. Add butter and beat to form a grainy paste. Scrape down sides of bowl, then add eggs and vanilla. Beat at medium speed until light and fluffy.
- Add the flour mixture and chocolate chips, and blend at low speed just until combined. Do not overmix.
- Drop dough by rounded tablespoons onto ungreased cookie sheets, 1½ inches apart. Bake for 18 to 22 minutes. Immediately transfer cookies with a spatula to a cool, flat surface.

Mandarin and Marmalade Cookies

2 ¾ cups all-purpose flour
1 teaspoon baking powder
2 sticks (1 cup) salted butter, softened
1 cup granulated sugar
1 large egg

½ cup orange marmalade
One 10-ounce can mandarin oranges,
drained and chopped

Yield: About 3 ½ dozen

- Preheat oven to 300°F.
- In a medium bowl, combine flour and baking powder. Mix well with a wire whisk and set aside.
- In a large bowl, blend butter and sugar with an electric mixer to form a grainy paste. Add egg and orange marmalade, and beat at medium speed until smooth. Add the flour mixture and the oranges, and blend at low speed just until combined. Do not overmix.
- Drop by rounded tablespoons onto ungreased baking sheets, 1½ inches apart. Bake 18 to 22 minutes or until the bottoms of cookies begin to brown. Transfer the cookies with a spatula to a cool, flat surface.

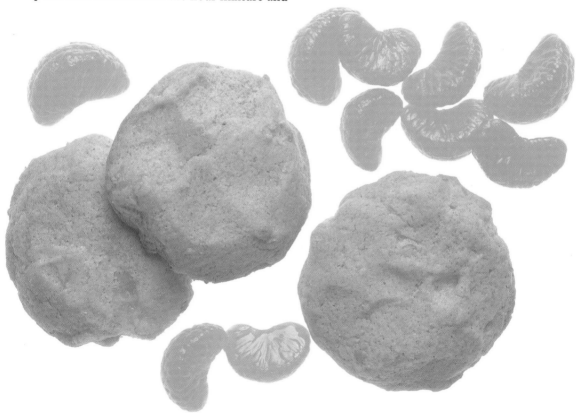

Best White Chocolate Butterscotch Cookies

2½ *cups all-purpose flour*
1 teaspoon baking soda
¼ *teaspoon salt*
2 sticks (1 cup) unsalted butter, softened
1½ *cups (packed) dark brown sugar*
2 large eggs
1 tablespoon light molasses

2 teaspoons vanilla extract
1 teaspoon Scotch whisky
1 cup chopped pecans, toasted
¾ *cup butterscotch chips*
¾ *cup white chocolate chips*

Yield: About 3 dozen

- Preheat the oven to 300°F.
- In a medium bowl, combine the flour, baking soda, and salt.
- In a large bowl with an electric mixer, cream the butter and sugar. Add the eggs, molasses, vanilla, and whisky, then blend well. Add the flour mixture and mix to blend. Stir in the pecans, butterscotch chips, and white chocolate chips. Do not overmix.
- Drop the cookie dough by rounded tablespoons 2 inches apart onto an ungreased cookie sheet. Bake for 18 to 20 minutes, or until set. Transfer to wire racks to cool.

Monster Chunk Cookies

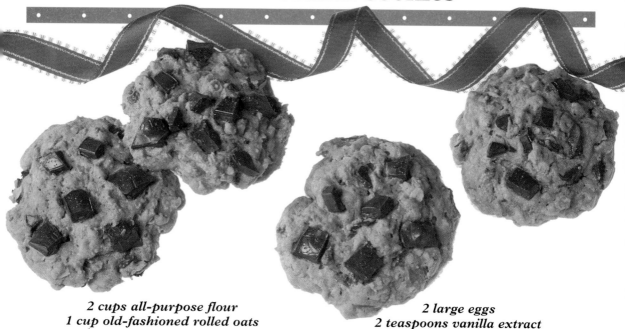

2 cups all-purpose flour
1 cup old-fashioned rolled oats
½ teaspoon baking soda
¼ teaspoon salt
2 sticks (1 cup) unsalted butter, softened
1⅓ cups (packed) dark brown sugar

2 large eggs
2 teaspoons vanilla extract
12 ounces semisweet chocolate, cut into
large chunks

Yield: 15 large cookies

- Preheat the oven to 300°F. In a medium bowl, combine the flour, oats, baking soda, and salt.
- In a large bowl with an electric mixer, cream the butter. Beat in the sugar and continue to beat until well combined. Beat in the eggs, one at a time, then add the vanilla. On low speed, blend in the flour mixture, stirring in the last bit with a wooden spoon. Stir in the chocolate chunks.

- Divide the dough into 15 equal portions. Place the portions of dough 3 inches apart on an ungreased cookie sheet and pat into disks ½ inch thick.
- Bake for 20 to 22 minutes, or until lightly browned on the underside. Cool on the cookie sheet for 1 minute, then carefully transfer to a wire rack to cool completely.

Before baking, press each mound of cookie dough to a ½-inch thickness.

Apricot Nectar Cookies

2¾ cups all-purpose flour
1 teaspoon baking soda
¾ cup granulated sugar
¼ cup (packed) dark brown sugar
2 sticks (1 cup) salted butter, softened
1 large egg

¼ cup apricot nectar
½ cup apricot preserves
¾ cup dried apricots, chopped

Yield: About 2 dozen

- Preheat oven to 300°F.
- In a medium bowl, combine flour and baking soda. Mix well with a wire whisk and set aside.
- In a large bowl, blend sugars with an electric mixer at medium speed. Add butter and mix to form a grainy paste. Scrape down sides of bowl. Then add egg, apricot nectar, and apricot preserves; beat at medium speed until smooth.
- Add the flour mixture and apricots, and blend on low just until combined. Do not overmix.
- Drop by rounded tablespoons onto ungreased baking sheets, 1½ inches apart. Bake 19 to 22 minutes or until cookies just begin to brown at bottom edges.
- Remove from oven and let cookies cool on baking sheets 5 minutes before transferring to a cool, flat surface with a spatula.

Cholesterol-Free Chocolate Chip Cookies

2½ cups all-purpose flour
½ teaspoon baking soda
¼ teaspoon salt
¾ cup (packed) dark brown sugar
½ cup granulated sugar
½ cup margarine
3 large egg whites

2 tablespoons honey
2 teaspoons vanilla extract
12 ounces semisweet chocolate chips
(about 2 cups)

Yield: About 3½ dozen

- Preheat oven to 300°F.
- In medium bowl, combine flour, soda, and salt. Mix well with a wire whisk and set aside.
- In a large bowl, blend sugars with an electric mixer. Add margarine and mix to form a grainy paste.
- In small bowl, beat egg whites until fluffy. Add egg whites, honey, and vanilla to sugar mixture, and beat until smooth. Scrape down the sides of the bowl.
- Add the flour mixture and chocolate chips, and blend on low speed just until combined. Do not overmix
- Drop by rounded tablespoons onto ungreased cookie sheets, 1½ inches apart. Bake for 15 to 18 minutes until lightly browned. Immediately transfer cookies with a spatula to a cool, flat surface.

Lacy Oatmeal Cookies

1 cup quick oats
¼ cup all-purpose flour
½ teaspoon salt
1½ teaspoons baking powder
1 cup granulated sugar

1 stick (½ cup) salted butter, softened
1 large egg
1 teaspoon vanilla extract

Yield: About 8 dozen

- Preheat oven to 325°F. Cover baking sheets with foil, then coat with nonstick vegetable spray.
- In a medium bowl, combine oats, flour, salt, and baking powder. Mix well with a wire whisk and set aside.
- In a large bowl, combine sugar and butter with an electric mixer at medium speed to form a grainy paste. Add egg and vanilla, and beat until smooth. Add flour mixture and blend just until combined.
- Drop dough by teaspoons onto baking sheets, 2½ inches apart. Bake for 9 to 12 minutes or until edges begin to turn golden brown. Let cool, then peel off cookies with your fingers.
- Be sure to respray the baking sheets between batches.

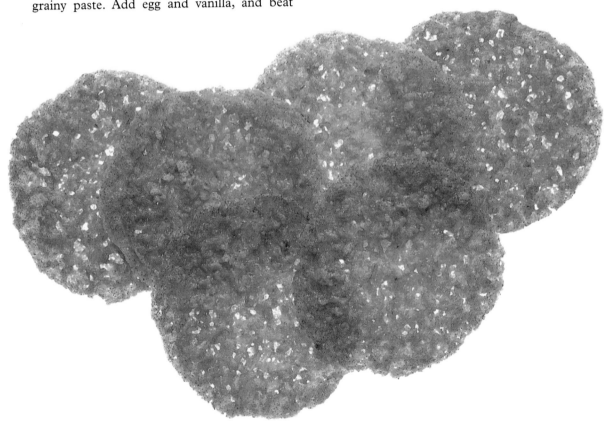

Cocomia Cookies

2 cups all-purpose flour
½ teaspoon baking soda
¼ teaspoon salt
¾ cup (packed) brown sugar
½ cup granulated sugar
1½ sticks (¾ cup) salted butter, softened
2 large eggs

2 teaspoons vanilla extract
6 ounces shredded, unsweetened coconut
(about 1 cup)
7 ounces whole macadamia nuts
(about 1½ cups)

Yield: About 3 dozen

- Preheat oven to 300°F.
- In a medium bowl, combine flour, soda, and salt. Mix well with a wire whisk and set aside.
- In a large bowl, blend sugars with an electric mixer at medium speed. Add butter and mix to form a grainy paste. Scrape down sides of bowl, then add eggs and vanilla. Beat at medium speed until light and fluffy.

- Add the flour mixture, the coconut, and macadamia nuts, and blend at low speed just until combined. Do not overmix.
- Drop by rounded tablespoons onto ungreased cookie sheets, 2 inches apart. Bake for 22 to 24 minutes. Immediately transfer cookies with a spatula to a cool, flat surface.

Chippity Chippers

2¾ cups cake flour
1 teaspoon baking soda
½ teaspoon salt
2 sticks (1 cup) unsalted butter, softened
½ cup (packed) light brown sugar
½ cup granulated sugar
1 tablespoon honey
2 large eggs
2 teaspoons vanilla extract

6 ounces semisweet chocolate chips
(about 1 cup)
6 ounces milk chocolate chips
(about 1 cup)
6 ounces white chocolate chips
(about 1 cup)
3 ounces peanut butter chips
(about ½ cup)

Yield: About 3 dozen

- Preheat the oven to 325°F.
- In a medium bowl, combine the flour, baking soda, and salt.
- In another medium bowl, cream the butter, sugars, and honey. Add the eggs one at a time, beating well after each addition. Beat in the vanilla. Stir in the flour mixture and all of the chips. Stir just until blended; do not overmix.
- Drop the dough by rounded tablespoons 2 inches apart on an ungreased cookie sheet. Bake for 18 to 20 minutes. Transfer to wire racks to cool.

Chocolate Chip Cookies with Toasted Pecans

2½ cups all-purpose flour
1 teaspoon baking soda
¼ teaspoon salt
2 sticks (1 cup) unsalted butter, softened
1 cup (packed) dark brown sugar
½ cup granulated sugar
2 large eggs

2 teaspoons vanilla extract
1 cup chopped pecans, toasted
12 ounces semisweet chocolate chips
(about 2 cups)

Yield: About 3 dozen

- Preheat the oven to 300°F.
- In a medium bowl, combine the flour, baking soda, and salt.
- In a large bowl with an electric mixer, cream the butter and sugars. Beat in the eggs and vanilla until just combined.

- Add the flour mixture, toasted pecans, and chocolate chips, then beat on low speed until just blended.
- Drop the dough by rounded tablespoons 2 inches apart on an ungreased cookie sheet. Bake for 15 to 20 minutes, or until golden. Transfer to wire racks to cool.

Applesauce Oaties

1¾ cups quick oats
1½ cups all-purpose flour
1 teaspoon baking powder
½ teaspoon baking soda
½ teaspoon salt
1 teaspoon ground cinnamon
½ teaspoon ground nutmeg
1 cup (packed) light brown sugar
½ cup granulated sugar

1 stick (½ cup) salted butter, softened
1 large egg
¾ cup applesauce
6 ounces semisweet chocolate chips
(about 1 cup)
6 ounces raisins (about 1 cup)
4 ounces chopped walnuts (about 1 cup)

Yield: About 4 dozen

- Preheat oven to 375°F.
- In a medium bowl, combine oats, flour, baking powder, soda, salt, cinnamon, and nutmeg. Mix well with a wire whisk and set aside.
- In a large bowl, combine sugars with an electric mixer at medium speed. Add butter and beat to form a grainy paste. Add egg and applesauce, and blend until smooth.
- Add the flour mixture, chocolate chips, raisins, and walnuts. Blend at low speed just until combined. Do not overmix.
- Drop dough by tablespoons onto lightly greased baking sheets, 2 inches apart. Bake 12 to 14 minutes or until cookies are light brown. Immediately transfer them with a spatula to a cool, flat surface.

Creamy Lemon Macadamia Cookies

2 cups all-purpose flour
1 teaspoon baking soda
¼ teaspoon salt
1 cup (packed) light brown sugar
½ cup granulated sugar
1 stick (½ cup) salted butter, softened
4 ounces cream cheese, softened

1 large egg
2 teaspoons lemon extract
7 ounces whole macadamia nuts
(about 1½ cups)

Yield: About 2½ dozen

- Preheat oven to 300°F.
- In a medium bowl, combine flour, soda, and salt. Mix well with wire whisk. Set aside.
- In a large bowl, blend sugars well with an electric mixer set at medium speed. Add the butter and cream cheese, and mix to form a smooth paste. Add the egg and lemon extract, and beat at medium speed until fully combined. Scrape down sides of bowl occasionally.
- Add the flour mixture and macadamia nuts. Blend at low speed just until combined. Do not overmix.
- Drop by rounded tablespoons onto ungreased cookie sheets, 2 inches apart. Bake 18 to 20 minutes. Immediately transfer cookies with a spatula to a cool, flat surface.

Krispies

2 cups all-purpose flour
1/4 teaspoon salt
1/2 teaspoon baking soda
1/2 cup (packed) dark brown sugar
1/2 cup granulated sugar
1 1/2 sticks (3/4 cup) salted butter, softened
1 large egg

2 teaspoons vanilla extract
1 cup crispy rice cereal
8 ounces crispy rice chocolate bar, coarsely
chopped (about 1 1/2 cups)

Yield: About 3 dozen

- Preheat oven to 300°F.
- In a medium bowl, combine flour, salt, and soda. Mix well with a wire whisk and set aside.
- In a large bowl, blend sugars with an electric mixer at medium speed. Add butter and mix to form a grainy paste. Scrape down sides of bowl, then add egg and vanilla. Beat at medium speed until light and fluffy.

- Add flour mixture, rice cereal, and chocolate chunks. Blend at low speed just until combined. Do not overmix.
- Drop by rounded tablespoons onto ungreased cookie sheets, 2 inches apart. Bake for 18 to 20 minutes. Immediately transfer cookies with a spatula to a cool, flat surface.

Fudge Cookies with White Chocolate

12 ounces semisweet chocolate, finely
chopped
2 cups all-purpose flour
$^{3}/_{4}$ cup unsweetened cocoa powder
1 teaspoon baking soda
$^{1}/_{4}$ teaspoon salt
2 sticks (1 cup) unsalted butter, softened

$1^{1}/_{2}$ cups (packed) dark brown sugar
3 large eggs, at room temperature
2 teaspoons vanilla extract
4 ounces white chocolate, coarsely chopped
1 teaspoon vegetable oil

Yield: About 3 dozen

- Preheat the oven to 300°F.
- In a double boiler, melt the semisweet chocolate over hot, not simmering, water. Set aside to cool slightly.
- In a medium bowl, combine the flour, cocoa, baking soda, and salt.
- In a large bowl with an electric mixer, cream the butter and sugar. Beat in the eggs and vanilla until just combined. Blend in the cooled semisweet chocolate. Blend in the flour mixture until just combined.

- Drop the dough by rounded tablespoons 2 inches apart onto an ungreased cookie sheet. Bake for 18 to 22 minutes, or until set. Cool on the cookie sheet for 1 minute, then transfer to wire racks to cool completely.
- In a double boiler, melt the white chocolate with the oil over hot, not simmering, water. Set aside to cool slightly.
- Dip a fork into the melted white chocolate and drizzle over the cookies.

Nutty White Chunk Cookies

2¼ cups all-purpose flour
½ teaspoon baking soda
¼ teaspoon salt
1 cup (packed) light brown sugar
½ cup granulated sugar
1½ sticks (¾ cup) salted butter, softened
2 large eggs

2 teaspoons vanilla extract
4 ounces pecans, chopped (about 1 cup)
8 ounces white chocolate bar,
coarsely chopped (about 1½ cups)

Yield: About 3 dozen

- Preheat oven to 300°F.
- In medium bowl, combine flour, soda, and salt. Mix well with a wire whisk. Set aside.
- In large bowl with an electric mixer blend sugars at medium speed. Add butter and mix to form a grainy paste, scraping down the sides of the bowl. Add eggs and vanilla, and beat at medium speed until light and fluffy.
- Add the flour mixture, pecans, and white chocolate, and blend at low speed until just combined. Do not overmix.
- Drop by rounded tablespoons onto ungreased cookie sheets, 2 inches apart. Bake 20 to 22 minutes or until edges just begin to turn golden brown. Use a spatula to transfer cookies immediately to a cool, flat surface.

Pineapple Paradise Cookies

3 cups all-purpose flour
½ teaspoon baking soda
¾ cup (packed) dark brown sugar
¾ cup granulated sugar
2 sticks (1 cup) salted butter, softened
1 large egg
2 teaspoons vanilla extract

One 8-ounce can crushed pineapple or
1 cup fresh finely chopped pineapple,
well drained
1 tablespoon pineapple juice
¼ cup sweetened shredded coconut

Yield: About 3 dozen

- Preheat oven to 300°F.
- In medium bowl, combine flour and baking soda. Mix well with a wire whisk. Set aside.
- In large bowl with an electric mixer blend sugars. Add butter and mix to form a grainy paste, scraping down the sides of the bowl. Add egg, vanilla, crushed pineapple, and pineapple juice and beat on medium speed until smooth.
- Add the flour mixture and blend at low speed until just combined. Do not overmix.
- Drop by rounded tablespoons onto ungreased baking sheets, 2 inches apart. Sprinkle lightly with shredded coconut.
- Bake 22 to 24 minutes or until cookies begin to turn lightly brown at edges. Transfer immediately to a cool, flat surface with a spatula.

Butterscotch Pecan Cookies

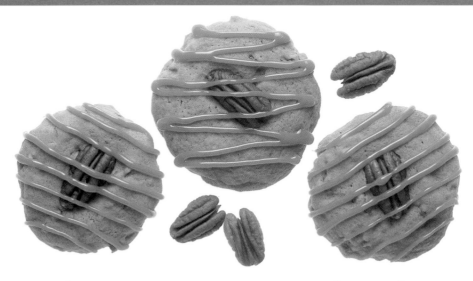

COOKIES
2½ cups all-purpose flour
½ teaspoon baking soda
¼ teaspoon salt
1½ cups (packed) dark brown sugar
2 sticks (1 cup) salted butter, softened
2 large eggs
2 teaspoons vanilla extract*
4 ounces chopped pecans (about 1 cup)
3 ounces whole pecans (about 1 cup)

CARAMEL GLAZE
8 ounces caramels
¼ cup heavy cream

Yield: About 2½ dozen

For an authentic butterscotch flavor, an equal quantity of Scotch whisky may be substituted for the vanilla.

- Preheat oven to 300°F.
- In medium bowl, combine flour, soda, and salt. Mix well with a wire whisk. Set aside.
- In large bowl with electric mixer beat sugar and butter. Mix to form a grainy paste, scraping down the sides of the bowl. Add eggs and vanilla, and beat at medium speed until soft and lumpy. Add the flour mixture and chopped pecans, and mix at low speed until just combined. Do not overmix.
- Drop dough by rounded tablespoons 2 inches apart onto ungreased cookie sheets. Place one whole pecan in center of each cookie. Bake 23 to 25 minutes or until cookie edges begin to brown lightly. Transfer immediately to cool, flat surface with a spatula.

- PREPARE THE CARAMEL GLAZE: Melt the caramels with the cream in a small saucepan over low heat. Stir with a wooden spoon until smooth. Remove from heat.
- Drizzle cooled cookies with caramel glaze into desired pattern using a spoon or fork.

Drizzle cookies with the caramel glaze for an extra touch of creamy flavor. Make sure that the glaze flows from the fork in a thin stream in order to achieve a decorative effect.

Lemon Poppy Seed Cookies

2 cups all-purpose flour	*1 cup granulated sugar*
½ teaspoon baking soda	*2 large egg yolks*
1½ teaspoons freshly grated lemon zest	*1 large whole egg*
1 teaspoon ground coriander	*1½ teaspoons lemon extract*
2 tablespoons poppy seeds	
1½ sticks (¾ cup) salted butter, softened	*Yield: About 2 dozen*

- Preheat oven 300°F.
- In a medium bowl, combine flour, baking soda, lemon zest, coriander, and poppy seeds. Mix well with a wire whisk and set aside.
- In a large bowl, cream butter and sugar with electric mixer at medium speed until mixture forms a grainy paste. Scrape down sides of bowl, then add yolks, egg, and lemon extract. Beat at medium speed until light and fluffy.

- Add the flour mixture and mix at low speed just until combined. Do not overmix.
- Drop by rounded tablespoons onto ungreased cookie sheets, 2 inches apart. Bake for 21 to 23 minutes until cookies are slightly brown along edges. Immediately transfer cookies with a spatula to a cool, flat surface.

Chocolate Coconut Crunch Cookies

2 cups all-purpose flour
1 teaspoon baking soda
¼ teaspoon salt
2 sticks (1 cup) unsalted butter, softened
¾ cup (packed) light brown sugar
¾ cup granulated sugar
2 large eggs, lightly beaten
2 teaspoons vanilla extract

1 teaspoon almond extract
2 cups shredded coconut
12 ounces semisweet chocolate chips
(about 2 cups)
1½ cups lightly salted, dry-roasted
almonds, finely chopped

Yield: About 4 dozen

- Preheat the oven to 300°F.
- In a small bowl, combine the flour, baking soda, and salt.
- In a medium bowl with an electric mixer, cream the butter and sugars. Beat in the eggs, vanilla, and almond extract. Mix on low speed until blended. Add the flour mixture and mix just until blended; do not overmix. Add the coconut, chocolate chips, and almonds and stir until just incorporated.
- Drop the dough by rounded tablespoons 2 inches apart onto an ungreased cookie sheet. Bake for 18 to 20 minutes, or until set. Transfer to wire racks to cool.

Chocolate Peanut Florentines

4 tablespoons (¼ cup) unsalted butter
¼ cup (packed) light brown sugar
¼ cup light corn syrup
⅓ cup all-purpose flour
½ cup finely chopped unsalted peanuts

1 teaspoon vanilla extract
4 ounces semisweet chocolate, finely
chopped

Yield: About 16 sandwich cookies

- Preheat the oven to 350°F. Butter and flour a cookie sheet.
- In a small saucepan, melt the butter over medium heat. Add the brown sugar and corn syrup and bring to a boil over medium heat, stirring constantly until the sugar dissolves, 3 to 5 minutes. Remove the pan from the heat and stir in the flour, peanuts, and vanilla.
- Quickly drop the batter in ½-teaspoon mounds 2 inches apart onto the prepared cookie sheet. Using a small spatula, spread each mound into an even circle.

- Bake for 9 to 10 minutes, or until browned; rotate the pan back to front halfway through the baking time. Cool on the cookie sheet for 1 to 2 minutes, then transfer to wire racks to cool completely.
- In a double boiler, melt the chocolate over hot, not simmering, water. Spread a thin layer of chocolate over the bottom (flat side) of one cookie. Cover with another cookie and gently press together. Repeat with the remaining cookies. Refrigerate the cookies to set the chocolate.

Soft and Chewy Peanut Butter Cookies

2 cups all-purpose flour
½ teaspoon baking soda
¼ teaspoon salt
1¼ cups (packed) dark brown sugar
1¼ cups granulated sugar
2 sticks (1 cup) salted butter, softened

3 large eggs
1 cup creamy peanut butter
2 teaspoons vanilla extract

Yield: About 3½ dozen

- Preheat oven to 300°F.
- In a medium bowl, combine flour, soda, and salt. Mix well with a wire whisk. Set aside.
- In a large bowl, blend sugars using an electric mixer set at medium speed. Add butter and mix to form a grainy paste, scraping the sides of the bowl. Add eggs, peanut butter, and vanilla, and mix at medium speed until light and fluffy.
- Add the flour mixture and mix at low speed until just mixed. Do not overmix.
- Drop by rounded tablespoons onto an ungreased cookie sheet, 1½ inches apart. With a wet fork, gently press a crisscross pattern on top of cookies. Bake for 18 to 22 minutes until cookies are slightly brown along edges. Transfer cookies immediately to a cool, flat surface with a spatula.
- As a variation, add 2 cups coarsely chopped semisweet chocolate bar or 2 cups semisweet chocolate chips to the flour mixture, then bake as directed.

After the dough is dropped onto the cookie sheet, use a fork to press a crisscross pattern in each cookie. In order to keep dough from sticking to the fork as you proceed, dip the fork in water after each cookie is flattened.

Oatmeal Raisin Chews

2¼ cups all-purpose flour
½ teaspoon baking soda
¼ teaspoon salt
1 cup quick oats (not instant)
1 cup (packed) dark brown sugar
½ cup granulated sugar
2 sticks (1 cup) salted butter, softened
2 tablespoons honey

2 teaspoons vanilla extract
2 large eggs
8 ounces raisins (about 1½ cups)
2 ounces walnuts, chopped (about ½ cup)
(optional)

Yield: About 2½ dozen without walnuts
About 3 dozen with walnuts

- Preheat oven to 300°F.
- In a medium bowl, combine flour, soda, salt, and oats. Mix well with wire whisk and set aside.
- In a large bowl, blend sugars with an electric mixer set at medium speed. Add butter and mix to form a grainy paste. Scrape down sides of bowl, then add honey, vanilla, and eggs. Mix at medium speed until light and fluffy.
- Add the flour mixture, raisins, and walnuts, if desired, and blend at low speed just until combined. Do not overmix.
- Drop by rounded tablespoons onto ungreased cookie sheets, 1½ inches apart. Bake for 18 to 22 minutes or until cookies are light golden brown. Immediately transfer cookies with a spatula to a cool, flat surface.

Pumpkin Spice Cookies

2½ cups all-purpose flour
½ teaspoon baking soda
¼ teaspoon salt
2 teaspoons pumpkin pie spice
1 cup (packed) dark brown sugar
½ cup granulated sugar
1½ sticks (¾ cup) salted butter, softened

1 large egg
1 cup pumpkin (canned or freshly cooked)
1 teaspoon vanilla extract
6 ounces raisins (about 1 cup)
2 ounces walnuts, chopped (about ½ cup)

Yield: About 3 dozen

- Preheat oven to 300°F.
- In a medium bowl, combine flour, soda, salt, and pumpkin pie spice. Mix well with a wire whisk and set aside.
- In a large bowl, blend sugars with an electric mixer set at medium speed. Add the butter and beat to form a grainy paste. Scrape sides of bowl, then add egg, pumpkin, and vanilla. Beat at medium speed until light and fluffy.
- Add the flour mixture, raisins, and walnuts. Blend at low speed just until combined. Do not overmix.
- Drop by rounded tablespoons onto ungreased cookie sheets, 1½ inches apart. Bake 22 to 24 minutes until cookies are slightly brown along edges. Immediately transfer cookies with a spatula to a cool, flat surface.

Chocolate Raisin Cookies

2 sticks (1 cup) salted butter, divided
2 ounces unsweetened baking chocolate
2¼ cups all-purpose flour
½ teaspoon baking soda
¼ teaspoon salt
1 cup (packed) dark brown sugar
½ cup granulated sugar

2 large eggs
2 teaspoons vanilla extract
9 ounces raisins (about 1½ cups)
6 ounces semisweet chocolate chips
(about 1 cup)

Yield: About 4 dozen

- Preheat oven to 300°F.
- In a double boiler over hot, not boiling water, melt ½ cup butter and the unsweetened chocolate. Remove from heat. Set aside.
- In medium bowl, combine flour, soda, and salt. Mix well with a wire whisk. Set aside.
- In large bowl with an electric mixer blend sugars at medium speed until fluffy. Add the remaining ½ cup butter and mix to form a grainy paste, scraping down the sides of the bowl. Add eggs and vanilla, and beat at medium speed until light and fluffy. Add melted chocolate and blend until the mixture is thoroughly combined.
- Add the flour mixture, raisins, and chocolate chips. Blend at low speed until just combined. Do not overmix.
- Drop by rounded tablespoons onto ungreased baking sheets, 2 inches apart. Bake for 20 to 22 minutes or until set. Transfer to a cool, flat surface immediately with a spatula.

Choc-Co-Chunks

2¼ cups all-purpose flour
1 teaspoon baking soda
1½ sticks (¾ cup) unsalted butter, softened
1 cup (packed) dark brown sugar
2 large eggs
2 teaspoons vanilla extract

1⅓ cups shredded coconut
12 ounces white chocolate, cut into chunks
1 cup coarsely chopped macadamia nuts

Yield: About 3 dozen

- Preheat the oven to 300°F.
- In a small bowl, combine the flour and baking soda.
- In a medium bowl with an electric mixer, cream the butter and sugar. Beat in the eggs and vanilla. Beat in the flour mixture; do not overmix. Stir in the coconut, white chocolate chunks, and macadamia nuts.
- Drop the dough by rounded tablespoons 2 inches apart onto an ungreased cookie sheet. Bake for 18 to 20 minutes. Transfer to a wire rack to cool.

Filled Cookies

Apple Cream Pennies

COOKIES
2½ cups all-purpose flour
½ teaspoon baking soda
¼ teaspoon salt
1 cup (packed) dark brown sugar
½ cup granulated sugar
2 sticks (1 cup) salted butter, softened
2 large eggs
2 teaspoons vanilla extract

FILLING
8 ounces cream cheese, softened
¼ cup granulated sugar
¼ cup apple butter

Yield: About 6 dozen

- Preheat oven to 300°F.
- In a medium bowl, combine flour, soda, and salt. Mix well with a wire whisk. Set aside.
- Blend sugars in a large bowl using an electric mixer set at medium speed. Add butter and mix to form a grainy paste, scraping down the sides of the bowl. Add eggs and vanilla, and beat at medium speed until light and fluffy.
- Add the flour mixture and blend at low speed until just combined. Do not overmix.
- Shape dough into marble-size balls. Place balls on ungreased baking sheets, 1 inch apart. Bake 10 to 11 minutes. Do not brown. Transfer cookies to a cool, flat surface with a spatula.
- PREPARE THE FILLING: Blend cream cheese and sugar in medium bowl with an electric mixer on medium until fluffy. Add apple butter and beat until filling is smooth and thoroughly combined.
- With a small knife spread 1 teaspoon of apple cream on the bottom half of each cooled cookie. Top with another cookie to create a sandwich. Repeat with remaining cookies and filling.

Jessica's Marshmallow Clouds

3 cups all-purpose flour
⅔ cup unsweetened cocoa powder
½ teaspoon baking soda
1 cup granulated sugar
1 cup (packed) light brown sugar
2 sticks (1 cup) salted butter, softened
2 large eggs

2 teaspoons vanilla extract
12 ounces mini semisweet chocolate chips
(about 2 cups)
8 ounces mini marshmallows, frozen

Yield: About 3½ dozen

- Preheat oven to 400°F. Until you are ready to assemble the cookies just prior to baking, keep the marshmallows in the freezer—otherwise they will thaw too rapidly.
- In a medium bowl, combine flour, cocoa, and baking soda. Set aside.
- Combine sugars in a large bowl. Using an electric mixer, blend in butter, scraping down the sides of the bowl. Add eggs and vanilla, and beat at medium speed until light and fluffy.

- Add the flour mixture and chocolate chips, and blend at low speed until combined. Batter will be very stiff.
- Gather 4 or 5 frozen marshmallows in the palm of your hand and cover them with a heaping tablespoon of dough. Wrap the dough around the marshmallows, completely encasing them and forming a 2-inch-diameter dough ball.
- Place balls on ungreased cookie sheets, 2 inches apart. Bake 8 to 10 minutes. Cool on pan 2 minutes, then transfer to a cool, flat surface.

Take 4 or 5 frozen mini marshmallows in the palm of your hand (far left). Spoon a heaping tablespoon of dough over the marshmallows and wrap them inside (left). Form a 2-inch ball, then place it on an ungreased cookie sheet.

Lemon Cream-Filled Cookies

COOKIES
1½ sticks (¾ cup) salted butter, softened
½ cup confectioners' sugar
2 teaspoons lemon extract
1½ cups all-purpose flour
¼ cup cornstarch

FILLING
½ stick (¼ cup) salted butter, softened
1 cup confectioners' sugar
1 tablespoon heavy cream
Juice of 1 freshly squeezed lemon
(about 2 tablespoons)
Grated zest of 1 lemon (2 to 3 teaspoons)

Yield: About 2 dozen

- MAKE THE COOKIE DOUGH: In a medium bowl, cream butter with an electric mixer set at medium speed. Add sugar and beat until smooth, scraping down sides of bowl as needed.
- Add lemon extract and beat until light and fluffy. Then add flour and cornstarch; blend at low speed until thoroughly combined.
- Gather dough into 2 balls of equal size and flatten into disks. Wrap the disks tightly in plastic wrap or a plastic bag. Refrigerate for 1 hour.
- MAKE THE FILLING: In a small bowl, beat butter with mixer until fluffy. Gradually add sugar while continuing to beat. Add cream, lemon juice, and lemon zest. Mix until thoroughly blended and set aside. To harden filling quickly, refrigerate for 15 to 20 minutes.

- At this point, preheat the oven to 325°F.
- Using a floured rolling pin, roll the chilled cookie dough on a floured board to a ¼-inch thickness. Cut circles with a 2-inch-diameter cookie cutter or drinking glass. Place circles of dough on ungreased cookie sheets, ½ inch apart. Continue rolling out and cutting dough scraps until all dough is used.
- Bake for 15 to 17 minutes, or until edges begin to brown. Immediately transfer cookies with a spatula to a cool, flat surface.
- When cookies are completely cool, spread a cookie with 1 teaspoon of the lemon cream. Place another cookie on top of the filling to make a sandwich. Complete entire batch.

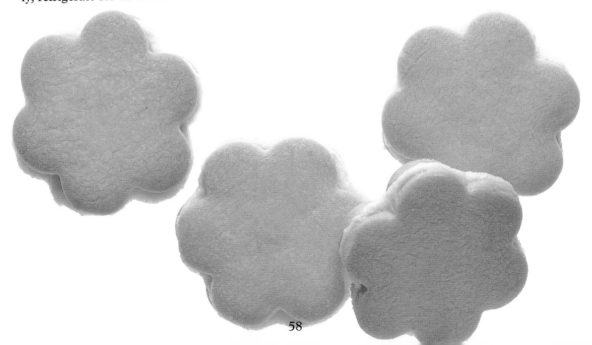

Chocolate Glazed Creamy Lemon Turnovers

PASTRY
2 cups all-purpose flour
2 tablespoons granulated sugar
½ teaspoon salt
1½ sticks (¾ cup) cold unsalted butter, cut into pieces
2 ounces cold cream cheese, cut into pieces
3 tablespoons ice water

LEMON FILLING
6 tablespoons unsalted butter
4 large egg yolks
1 large egg
¾ cup granulated sugar
¼ cup fresh lemon juice
2 teaspoons grated lemon peel

TOPPINGS
1 egg, beaten
Granulated sugar, for sprinkling
5 ounces semisweet chocolate chips
½ cup heavy cream

Yield: 2 dozen turnovers

- PREPARE THE PASTRY: In a medium bowl, combine the flour, sugar, and salt. With a pastry blender, incorporate the butter and cream cheese until the mixture is the size of small peas. With a fork, stir in the ice water. Gather the dough into a ball, flatten into a disk, wrap in plastic, and chill in the refrigerator for about 30 minutes.
- MAKE THE LEMON FILLING: In a double boiler, melt the butter. In a medium bowl, whisk together the egg yolks, egg, sugar, lemon juice, and lemon peel. Add the egg mixture to the butter and cook, stirring frequently, until the mixture thickens and heavily coats the back of a spoon, about 15 minutes. Transfer the filling to a small bowl and refrigerate until firm, about 2 hours.
- BAKE: Preheat the oven to 400°F. Cut the chilled dough in half and return half to the refrigerator. Roll the remaining half into a 12-by-16-inch rectangle. Cut into twelve 4-inch squares. Spoon about 1 tablespoon of filling into the center of each square. Moisten two adjacent sides of a pastry square with water, then fold the pastry over to form a triangle. Crimp the edges to seal. Brush each turnover with some of the beaten egg and cut three slits as steam vents. Sprinkle the tops with granulated sugar and place on an ungreased cookie sheet. Bake for 20 minutes, or until golden. Place on racks to cool to room temperature. Repeat with the remaining dough and filling.
- Meanwhile, make the chocolate glaze: Place the chocolate chips in a small bowl. In a small saucepan, bring the cream to a simmer. Pour the hot cream over the chocolate. Let stand, covered, for 5 minutes, then stir until smooth.

Pineapple Pocket Pies

COOKIES
1 cup all-purpose flour
½ cup whole-wheat flour
½ teaspoon baking soda
½ stick (¼ cup) salted butter, softened
¼ cup (packed) light brown sugar
¼ cup honey
1 large egg
1 teaspoon vanilla extract

FILLING
½ cup dried apricots
½ cup fresh or canned unsweetened pineapple, in chunks
¼ cup (packed) dark brown sugar
1½ cups water

Yield: 32 pockets

- In medium bowl, combine flours and soda. Mix well with a wire whisk. Set aside.
- In large bowl with an electric mixer combine butter and sugar at medium speed. Add honey, egg, and vanilla and beat at medium speed until smooth. Scrape down the sides of the bowl, then add the flour mixture. Blend at low speed until just combined; do not overmix.
- Gather dough into a ball. Divide in half and roll into two 6-inch cylinders. Wrap each cylinder tightly in plastic wrap or in a plastic bag. Refrigerate 1 hour.
- PREPARE THE FILLING: Combine all the filling ingredients in medium saucepan over medium-low heat and stir until sugar dissolves. Turn heat up to medium and simmer—stirring occasionally—until mixture thickens and most of the liquid evaporates. Remove from heat and allow mixture to cool to room temperature. Purée filling in food processor or blender.
- Preheat oven to 325°F. Using your hands, roll each cylinder out to about 12 inches in length. Then place 1 cylinder on a floured board and using a floured rolling pin, roll into a rectangle roughly 5 inches wide, 18 inches long, and ⅛ inch thick.
- Spread half of the filling mixture down the center of the dough in a ribbon about 2 inches wide. With a metal spatula, loosen the dough, and fold each side lengthwise over the filling, one side overlapping the other by ½ inch.
- Cut strip in half widthwise to make handling easier. Use spatula to transfer each 9-inch strip onto an ungreased baking sheet, turning the strips over so that the seams are on the bottom. Repeat procedure with remaining dough and filling.
- Bake 20 to 22 minutes or until dough begins to turn a light gold. Do not brown. Cool strips on sheet for 1 minute, then transfer to cool surface. When strips reach room temperature, cut each into 8 pieces with a thin, sharp knife.

Refrigerator Thumbprint Fudgy Cookies

½ stick (¼ cup) salted butter, softened
½ cup heavy cream
1 cup granulated sugar
1 teaspoon vanilla extract
12 ounces semisweet chocolate chips
(about 2 cups)

2½ cups quick oats (not instant)
1 cup raspberry preserves
¼ cup confectioners' sugar

Yield: About 2½ dozen

- In a 2-quart saucepan, combine butter, cream, and sugar. Warm over medium heat, stirring constantly, until sugar dissolves. Remove from heat, add vanilla and chocolate chips, 1 cup at a time, stirring until chocolate melts. To complete the dough, fold in the oats and stir until all ingredients are thoroughly combined.
- Shape dough into 1-inch balls and place on a cookie sheet lined with wax paper. Using the bottom of a glass, flatten cookies to 2 inches in diameter. Make a depression in center of each cookie with your thumb. Chill cookies in refrigerator 30 minutes or until set. Spoon ½ teaspoon of preserves into center of each cookie. Dust with confectioners' sugar.

Spoon the chocolate chips into the liquid ingredients 1 cup at a time (far left). Stir after each addition to ensure that the chips have melted. After all the chocolate has been incorporated, add the oats and stir until completely moistened (left).

Surprise-Filled Cookies

2½ *cups all-purpose flour*
½ *teaspoon baking powder*
2 sticks (1 cup) salted butter, softened
1 cup granulated sugar
1 large egg

2 teaspoons vanilla extract
1 cup fruit jam

Yield: About 4 dozen

- Preheat oven to 300°F.
- In medium bowl, combine flour and baking powder. Mix well with a wire whisk. Set aside.
- In another medium bowl with an electric mixer, cream butter and sugar. Add egg and vanilla, and beat on medium until smooth. Add the flour mixture and blend at low speed until thoroughly combined. Dough will be firm.
- Scoop tablespoonfuls of dough, roll into 1-inch-diameter balls, and place on ungreased baking sheets, 1 inch apart. With the small end of a melon baller, scoop out the center of the dough balls. Do not scoop all the way through the cookie. Place ½ teaspoon of jam in the center of each dough ball. Place scooped-out dough back into mixing bowl to use to form more cookies.
- Bake 22 to 24 minutes or until golden brown. Transfer to a cool, flat surface.

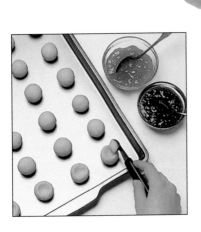

Use the smaller scoop of a melon baller to remove a small amount of dough from each ball. Spoon your favorite jams into the depression, then bake as directed.

Peanut Butter Cream-Filled Cookies

COOKIES

1½ cups all-purpose flour
½ teaspoon baking soda
½ teaspoon ground cinnamon
1 cup quick oats (not instant)
1 cup (packed) light brown sugar
1 stick (½ cup) salted butter, softened
1 large egg
1 teaspoon vanilla extract

FILLING

¾ cup creamy peanut butter
½ stick (¼ cup) salted butter, softened
2 tablespoons half-and-half
1 teaspoon vanilla extract
1½ cups confectioners' sugar

Yield: About 3½ dozen

- Preheat oven to 325°F.
- In medium bowl, combine flour, soda, cinnamon, and oats. Mix well with a wire whisk. Set aside.
- Cream sugar and butter in a large bowl using an electric mixer set at medium speed. Add egg and vanilla, and beat at medium speed until light and creamy. Add the flour-oat mixture, and blend at low speed until just combined. Do not overmix.
- Separate dough into 2 balls, flatten them into disks, and wrap each tightly in plastic wrap or a plastic bag. Chill 1 hour.
- On floured board using a floured rolling pin, roll out 1 disk to ¼-inch thickness. Cut cookies with a 2-inch round fluted cookie cutter dipped in flour. Repeat procedure with the second disk, reworking scraps until all the dough is used. Bake cookies on ungreased baking sheets ½ inch apart for 13 to 15 minutes or until bottoms turn light brown. Transfer immediately to a cool, flat surface with a spatula.
- When cookies are cool, spread 1 tablespoon of peanut butter filling on the bottom side of a cookie. Top with another cookie—bottom side toward the filling—to make a sandwich. Repeat with the remaining cookies and filling.

Use a cookie cutter dipped in flour to cut the cookies from the dough. This cookie cutter has a fluted edge—it makes a particularly attractive cookie.

Chocolate Cream-Filled Hearts

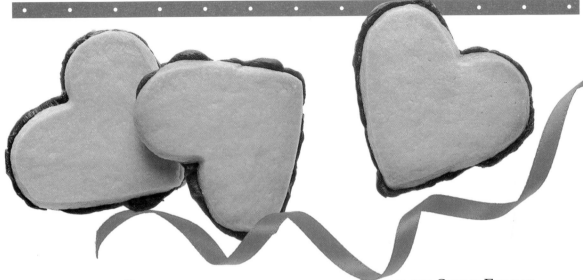

COOKIES
3 sticks (1½ cups) salted butter, softened
1½ cups confectioners' sugar
4 teaspoons vanilla extract
3 cups all-purpose flour

CHOCOLATE CREAM FILLING
½ cup heavy cream
6 ounces semisweet chocolate chips
(about 1 cup)

TOPPING
¼ cup confectioners' sugar (optional)

Yield: About 2½ dozen

- Cream butter in a medium bowl with electric mixer set at medium speed. Add 1½ cups confectioners' sugar and beat until smooth. Add vanilla and mix until creamy. Scrape bowl. Add flour and mix at low speed until thoroughly mixed.
- Gather dough into 2 balls and flatten to disks. Wrap dough tightly in plastic wrap or place in an airtight plastic bag. Refrigerate for 1 hour or until firm.
- Preheat oven to 325°F.
- Using a floured rolling pin, roll dough on floured board to ¼-inch thickness. Cut out 2-inch hearts with cookie cutters. Continue using dough scraps, rerolling and recutting until all dough is used. Be careful not to overwork the dough.
- Place cookies on ungreased cookie sheets, ½ inch apart. Bake 16 to 18 minutes or until firm. Transfer to cool, flat surface with spatula.

- PREPARE THE CHOCOLATE CREAM FILLING: Scald the cream in a small saucepan and remove from heat. Stir in the chocolate chips and cover for 15 minutes. Stir chocolate cream until smooth, then transfer to a small bowl. Set filling aside and let it cool to room temperature.
- Spread 1 teaspoon of chocolate filling on the bottom side of half of the cookies. Top with bottom side of another cookie, forming a sandwich. Repeat with remaining cookies and cream.
- If you wish, sift confectioners' sugar over the finished cookies.

Spread the chocolate filling on the bottom side of one cookie heart. Top with another heart, bottom side also touching the chocolate.

Chocolate Sandwich Cookies

COOKIES

1½ sticks (¾ cup) salted butter, softened
¾ cup confectioners' sugar
2 teaspoons vanilla extract
¼ cup unsweetened cocoa powder
2 tablespoons cornstarch
1 cup all-purpose flour

CREAM FILLING

1 stick (½ cup) salted butter, softened
1 cup confectioners' sugar
2 teaspoons vanilla extract
1 tablespoon heavy cream

Yield: About 1½ dozen

- In a medium bowl, cream butter with an electric mixer at medium speed. Add sugar and beat until smooth. Add vanilla and beat at medium speed until light and fluffy. In another bowl, combine the cocoa, cornstarch, and flour, and mix well with a wire whisk. Add the cocoa mixture to the wet ingredients and mix at low speed until thoroughly combined.
- Gather dough into a ball and flatten into a disk. Wrap dough tightly in plastic wrap or place in an airtight plastic bag. Refrigerate for 1½ hours or until firm.
- Preheat oven to 325°F.

- Using a floured rolling pin, roll dough on floured board to ¼-inch thickness. Cut shapes with cookie cutters and place on ungreased cookie sheets, 1 inch apart. Continue using dough scraps, rerolling and cutting until all dough is used. Be careful not to overwork the dough. Bake 16 to 18 minutes or until firm. Transfer cookies to a cool, flat surface with a spatula.
- PREPARE THE CREAM FILLING: Cream butter in a small bowl with an electric mixer set at medium speed. Add sugar, vanilla, and cream, and beat until smooth.

Custard-Filled Cookies

CUSTARD
1 cup sweetened condensed milk
One ½-inch piece vanilla bean, split
lengthwise, or 1 teaspoon vanilla extract
2 large egg yolks, at room temperature

COOKIES
1 stick (½ cup) salted butter, softened
½ cup granulated sugar
1 large egg

2 tablespoons heavy cream
1½ cups all-purpose flour

TOPPINGS
1 teaspoon ground cinnamon or
1 teaspoon confectioners' sugar or
1 teaspoon cocoa powder

Yield: About 1½ dozen

- In a medium saucepan over medium heat, heat condensed milk with vanilla bean or vanilla extract until small bubbles form on surface.
- Whisk egg yolks in a medium bowl. Stirring constantly, slowly add ½ cup of the hot milk to the egg yolks. Add the tempered egg yolks to the milk mixture in the saucepan. Stirring constantly with a metal spoon or whisk, cook for 5 minutes or until custard heavily coats the back of a spoon. Be careful not to let the custard boil.
- Strain custard through a sieve. Refrigerate until thoroughly chilled.
- Preheat oven to 325°F.

- PREPARE THE COOKIES: Mix butter and sugar in medium bowl with electric mixer at medium speed. Add egg and cream and mix until thoroughly blended. Scrape sides of bowl. Add the flour and blend on low speed just until combined. Do not overmix.
- Shape dough into 1-inch balls and place on ungreased cookie sheets 1 inch apart. With your thumb or the back of a small spoon, form a small depression in center of each ball.
- Bake 15 to 17 minutes or until bottoms begin to brown. Transfer cookies to cool, flat surface. When cookies cool to room temperature, spoon or pipe in 1½ teaspoons of chilled thickened custard. Sprinkle with ground cinnamon, confectioners' sugar, or cocoa, if desired.

Temper the beaten egg yolks by adding about ½ cup of the hot milk to the yolks, briskly whisking as you pour. This will warm the eggs enough so that when you add them to the hot milk, they will not become scrambled eggs.

Linzer Cookies

COOKIES
1½ cups all-purpose flour
½ cup ground almonds
½ teaspoon baking powder
½ teaspoon salt
½ teaspoon ground cinnamon
1½ sticks (¾ cup) salted butter, softened
¾ cup granulated sugar
2 egg yolks
1 teaspoon vanilla extract
1 teaspoon almond extract

FILLING
½ cup raspberry jam
1 teaspoon grated lemon peel
(½ of 1 medium lemon)

TOPPING
¼ cup confectioners' sugar
2 ounces sliced almonds (about ½ cup)

Yield: About 2 dozen

- Preheat oven to 300°F.
- Combine flour, almonds, baking powder, salt, and cinnamon with wire whisk.
- In large bowl with an electric mixer cream butter and sugar. Add egg yolks and the vanilla and almond extracts, and beat at medium speed until light and fluffy. Add the flour mixture and blend at low speed until just combined. Do not overmix.

- Roll dough into 1½-inch balls. Place 2 inches apart on ungreased baking sheets. With your index finger press an indentation in center of each ball to hold the filling.
- Bake 22 to 24 minutes or until just golden brown on bottom. Transfer cookies to a cool, flat surface with a spatula.
- In a small bowl, combine jam and grated lemon peel. Sift confectioners' sugar over cookies. Place ½ teaspoon of filling mixture in center of cooled cookie and place sliced almonds in the jam filling.

Once the cookies are cool, lightly dust them with confectioners' sugar (far left). Next, spoon the raspberry jam into the depression in each cookie. To finish off, arrange sliced almonds on top of the jam (left).

Fruit-Filled Jewels

1½ sticks (¾ cup) salted butter, softened
½ cup confectioners' sugar
2 large egg yolks
1 teaspoon vanilla extract

1½ cups all-purpose flour
1 cup any fruit jam

Yield: About 2 dozen

- Preheat oven to 325°F.
- In a medium bowl, cream butter with an electric mixer set at medium speed. Add sugar and beat until smooth. Add egg yolks and vanilla, and beat at medium speed until light and fluffy. Add the flour and blend at low speed until thoroughly combined.
- Gather dough into a ball and flatten to a disk. Wrap dough tightly in plastic wrap or place in plastic bag. Refrigerate for 1 hour.
- Using a floured rolling pin, roll dough on floured board to ¼-inch thickness. Cut circles with a 2-inch-diameter cookie cutter or drinking glass, and place on ungreased cookie sheets, 1 inch apart. Continue using dough scraps, rerolling and cutting until all the dough is used.
- Drop ½ teaspoon of fruit jam in center of each cookie, then top with another cookie. Using the tines of a fork, seal edges of cookies as shown.
- Bake for 15 to 17 minutes or until edges begin to brown.

Chocolate Dreams

COOKIES
1½ sticks (¾ cup) salted butter, softened
½ cup confectioners' sugar
¼ cup (packed) light brown sugar
2 large egg yolks
1 teaspoon vanilla extract
1½ cups all-purpose flour

CHOCOLATE FILLING
½ cup heavy cream
6 ounces semisweet chocolate chips
(about 1 cup)

TOPPING
2 tablespoons granulated sugar

Yield: About 2½ dozen

- In a medium bowl, cream butter using an electric mixer set at medium speed. Add confectioners' and brown sugars and beat until smooth. Add yolks and vanilla, and mix at medium speed until light and fluffy. Scrape bowl. Add the flour and blend at low speed until thoroughly combined.
- Gather dough into a ball and flatten to a disk. Wrap dough tightly in plastic wrap or place in plastic bag. Refrigerate for 1 hour.
- PREPARE THE FILLING: Scald the cream in a small saucepan over medium heat. Add the chocolate chips and stir until melted. Remove from the heat.
- Preheat oven to 325°F.
- Using a floured rolling pin, roll dough on floured board to ¼-inch thickness. Cut circles with a 2-inch-diameter cookie cutter and place on ungreased cookie sheets, 1 inch apart. Continue using dough scraps, rerolling and cutting until all dough is used. Drop 1 teaspoon of chocolate filling in center of each circle and top with another circle. Completely seal the edges using the tines of a fork. Bake 15 to 16 minutes, or until cookies are golden brown. Transfer cookies to a cool, flat surface with a metal spatula. Sprinkle with granulated sugar.

Spoon a heaping teaspoonful of chocolate filling into the center of each circle (far left). Cover each with another circle of dough and completely seal the edges with a fork (left).

Glazed Honey-Nut Rolls

FILLING AND HONEY GLAZE
³⁄₄ cup clover honey
¹⁄₃ cup water
1 teaspoon fresh lemon juice
1 cinnamon stick
8 ounces walnuts, coarsely chopped
4 ounces raisins (about ³⁄₄ cup)
1 teaspoon vanilla extract
¹⁄₄ teaspoon almond extract
6 ounces semisweet chocolate chips
(about 1 cup)

ASSEMBLY
10 sheets (13 by 22 inches) frozen phyllo
dough (about ¹⁄₄ pound), thawed
1 stick (¹⁄₂ cup) unsalted butter, melted

CHOCOLATE GLAZE
¹⁄₃ cup heavy cream
4 ounces semisweet chocolate chips

Confectioners' sugar, for dusting

Yield: About 20 nut rolls

- PREPARE THE FILLING: In a small saucepan, combine the honey, water, lemon juice, and cinnamon. Simmer for 10 minutes. Keep warm.
- In a medium bowl, combine the walnuts, raisins, vanilla, almond extract, and ¹⁄₂ cup of the honey mixture. Stir in the chocolate chips and set aside.
- ASSEMBLE AND BAKE: Preheat the oven to 375°F. Keeping the rest of the phyllo covered with plastic wrap and a damp towel, lay a sheet of dough on a work surface. Cut in half crosswise. Brush each half with melted butter. With a short end facing you, spoon about 1½ tablespoons of filling onto the phyllo. Fold in the sides and roll up the dough. Brush the rolls with more butter and place on a cookie sheet. Repeat with the remaining dough, filling, and

butter. Bake for 20 minutes, or until golden. Transfer to wire racks to cool, but immediately brush the rolls with the remaining honey glaze.
- MAKE THE CHOCOLATE GLAZE: In a small saucepan, bring the cream to a simmer. Remove from the heat, add the chips, and let stand for 5 minutes; stir until smooth. Let cool, then drizzle over the nut rolls. Dust the rolls with confectioners' sugar.

With a short end of the phyllo facing you, place about 1½ tablespoons of the filling about 1 inch in from the end. Fold in the sides of the dough and roll up.

Fancy Cookies

Almond Crunch Cookies

1 stick (¹⁄₂ cup) salted butter, softened
³⁄₄ cup granulated sugar
1 large egg
¹⁄₂ teaspoon almond extract
1 ounce almonds, ground in blender or
food processor (about ¹⁄₄ cup)
4 ounces sliced almonds (about 1 cup)

1 cup all-purpose flour
¹⁄₄ cup heavy cream
6 ounces semisweet chocolate chips
(about 1 cup)
2 teaspoons light corn syrup

Yield: About 1¹⁄₂ dozen

- Preheat oven to 350°F.
- In a medium bowl, blend butter and sugar with an electric mixer until mixture forms a grainy paste. Scrape down sides of bowl, then add egg and almond extract. Beat at medium speed until light and fluffy.
- Add the ground almonds and flour, and blend at low speed just until combined. Do not overmix. Form dough into 1¹⁄₂-inch balls and roll in sliced almonds, coating each ball thoroughly.
- Place balls on ungreased cookie sheets, 2 inches apart. Bake for 15 to 18 minutes or until cookies are slightly brown along edges. Immediately transfer cookies to a cool surface covered with wax paper.
- MAKE THE CHOCOLATE GLAZE: Scald cream in a small saucepan, then remove from heat. Stir in chocolate chips and corn syrup; cover and let stand for 15 minutes. With small wire whisk or wooden spoon, gently mix glaze until smooth, being careful not to create bubbles in the chocolate.
- When cookies are completely cool, drizzle patterns on them with the warm chocolate glaze, or dip half of each cookie into the glaze. Refrigerate the cookies on the wax paper until the glaze has set—about 10 minutes.

Roll dough lightly between your hands into 1¹⁄₂-inch balls (far left). The less you handle these cookies the lighter they will be. Then roll each ball in sliced almonds until fully coated (left).

Molasses Raisin Cookies

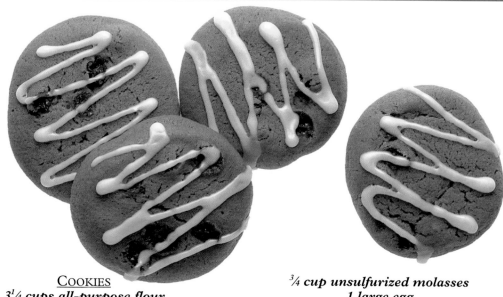

COOKIES
3¼ cups all-purpose flour
1 teaspoon baking soda
¼ teaspoon salt
2 teaspoons ground cinnamon
1 teaspoon ground ginger
½ teaspoon allspice
1 cup (packed) dark brown sugar
2 sticks (1 cup) salted butter, softened

¾ cup unsulfurized molasses
1 large egg
6 ounces raisins (about 1½ cups)

ICING
1 cup confectioners' sugar
2 tablespoons milk

Yield: About 4 dozen

- Preheat oven to 300°F.
- In a medium bowl, combine flour, soda, salt, cinnamon, ginger, and allspice. Mix well with a wire whisk and set aside.
- In a large bowl, beat sugar and butter with an electric mixer at medium speed until mixture forms a grainy paste. Scrape sides of bowl, then add molasses and egg. Beat until light and fluffy.
- Add the flour mixture and raisins, and blend at low speed just until combined. Do not overmix.
- Divide dough in half and shape each half into a roll 1½ inches in diameter. Wrap rolls in wax paper and refrigerate until firm, about 2 hours.
- Slice cookies ½ inch thick and place on ungreased cookie sheets, 1½ inches apart. Bake for 25 to 27 minutes until cookies are set. Immediately transfer cookies with a spatula to a cool surface.
- PREPARE THE ICING: Blend sugar and milk in a small bowl until smooth. Using a small spoon or knife, drizzle cookies with icing.

Unwrap the chilled rolls of dough and slice with a sharp knife into ½-inch-thick cookies. Place on ungreased cookie sheet.

Macadamia Nut Coconut Crisps

1 cup all-purpose flour
4 ounces raw macadamia nuts, coarsely
chopped (about 1 cup)
½ cup shredded sweetened coconut
1 stick (½ cup) salted butter, softened
½ cup light corn syrup

½ cup (packed) dark brown sugar
2 teaspoons vanilla extract
2 ounces mini semisweet chocolate chips
(about ⅓ cup)

Yield: About 3 dozen

- Preheat oven to 375°F.
- Combine flour, nuts, and coconut in a medium bowl. Set aside.
- Heat butter, corn syrup, and brown sugar in a 2-quart saucepan until boiling, stirring occasionally. Remove saucepan from heat and stir in vanilla. Add flour mixture and set aside to cool. Then add the chocolate chips and mix until all ingredients are equally distributed.

- Drop by half teaspoons onto well-greased cookie sheets, 2 inches apart. Bake 8 to 10 minutes or until the mixture spreads and bubbles.
- Cool cookies for 1 minute on cookie sheet, then immediately transfer to a cool, flat surface with a metal spatula. Cookies will remain soft until completely cooled.

Gently spoon the dry ingredients into the heated butter-and-sugar mixture (far left). Stir after every few spoonfuls until the dry ingredients are well incorporated (left).

Maple Pecan Butter Balls

1¼ cups all-purpose flour
½ teaspoon baking soda
1 teaspoon ground cinnamon
3 ounces pecans, finely ground in food
processor or blender (about ¾ cup)
1 stick (½ cup) salted butter, softened

⅔ cup granulated sugar
¼ cup pure maple syrup
1 large egg

Yield: About 2 dozen

- Preheat oven to 300°F.
- In a medium bowl, combine flour, soda, cinnamon, and finely ground pecans. (For extra flavor, sauté pecans in 1 tablespoon butter until slightly browned.) Mix ingredients well with a wire whisk and set aside.
- In another medium bowl, cream butter and sugar with an electric mixer set at medium speed until mixture forms a grainy paste. Add syrup and egg and beat until slightly thickened.
- Add the flour mixture and blend at low speed just until combined. Do not overmix. Place dough in a plastic bag and refrigerate until firm, about 1 hour.
- Remove dough from refrigerator and shape into 1-inch balls. Place cookies on ungreased cookie sheets, 1 inch apart. Bake 17 to 18 minutes, or until the cookie bottoms are golden brown. Immediately transfer the cookies with a spatula to a cool, flat surface.

To make cookies more festive, sprinkle them with confectioners' sugar using a small mesh sieve (far left). Then, spoon chocolate icing into a pastry bag fitted with a small (#3) plain tip. Pipe decorative patterns onto cookies as shown (left).

Gingerbread Men

COOKIES

3¼ cups all-purpose flour
½ teaspoon baking soda
¼ teaspoon salt
1 teaspoon ground cinnamon
2 teaspoons ground ginger
¼ teaspoon ground cloves
2 sticks (1 cup) salted butter, softened
¾ cup (packed) dark brown sugar
1 large egg

½ cup unsulfurized molasses
3 ounces raisins (about ½ cup) (optional)

ICING

⅔ cup confectioners' sugar
1 to 2 teaspoons milk

Yield: About 2½ dozen 6-inch cookies
About 3½ dozen 4-inch cookies

- Preheat oven to 325°F.
- Combine flour, soda, salt, cinnamon, ginger, and cloves in a medium bowl.
- In large bowl with an electric mixer cream butter and sugar. Scrape down the sides of the bowl. Add egg and molasses, and beat on medium speed until smooth. Scrape bowl and add the flour mixture. Blend on low speed just until combined; do not overmix.
- Separate dough into 2 balls and flatten into disks. Wrap each disk tightly in plastic wrap or a plastic bag, and refrigerate 1 hour or until firm.
- On floured surface with floured rolling pin, roll dough out to ¼-inch thickness. With floured cookie cutters, cut into gingerbread men.

Gather scraps and reroll dough until all dough is used. Place on ungreased baking sheets ½ inch apart.
- If you want to use raisins to decorate the cookies, plump raisins first by soaking them in warm water for 5 minutes. Discard water. Use raisins as eyes, mouths, and buttons.
- Bake 9 to 11 minutes being careful not to brown. Transfer to a cool, flat surface with a spatula.
- PREPARE THE ICING: Whisk sugar and milk together in a small bowl until mixture is smooth but liquid. If it seems dry, add ¼ teaspoon more milk. Spoon icing into a pastry bag fitted with a small piping tip. Decorate gingerbread men as desired.

Christmas Sugar Cookies

2 cups all-purpose flour
¼ teaspoon salt
1½ sticks (¾ cup) salted butter, softened
¾ cup granulated sugar
1 large egg

1 teaspoon vanilla extract
Colored sugars or sprinkles

Yield: About 3 dozen

- Preheat oven to 325°F.
- In a medium bowl, combine the flour and salt with a wire whisk.
- In a large bowl, cream the butter and sugar with an electric mixer on medium speed. Add the egg and vanilla, and beat until well mixed. Scrape down sides of bowl, then add the flour mixture. Blend on low speed just until combined. Do not overmix.
- Gather dough into a ball. Flatten the ball into a disk and wrap tightly in plastic wrap or a plastic bag. Refrigerate 1 hour or until firm.
- On a floured surface, roll out dough to a ¼-inch thickness. With cookie cutters, cut dough into desired shapes and place on ungreased cookie sheets. Decorate with colored sugars or sprinkles.
- Bake for 13 to 15 minutes, being careful not to brown. Immediately transfer cookies with a spatula to a cool, flat surface.

Brown Sugar Shortbread

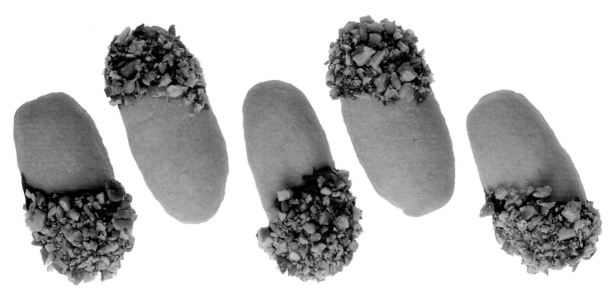

SHORTBREAD
2 sticks (1 cup) salted butter, softened
¾ cup (packed) light brown sugar
2 teaspoons vanilla extract
2 cups all-purpose flour

TOPPING
1 tablespoon salted butter
6 ounces semisweet chocolate chips
(about 1 cup)
4 ounces pecans, finely chopped
(about 1 cup)

Yield: About 2½ dozen

- Preheat oven to 325°F.
- In a large bowl, cream butter and sugar with an electric mixer at medium speed. Scrape down sides of bowl. Then add vanilla and flour, and blend thoroughly on low speed.
- Shape level tablespoons of dough into 1-inch balls, then form into logs 2 inches long and 1 inch wide. Place on ungreased baking sheets, 2 inches apart.
- Bake for 17 to 19 minutes, or until cookies spread, and turn a light golden brown. Transfer to a cool, flat surface.
- MAKE TOPPING: Melt butter and chocolate chips in a double boiler over hot, not boiling, water, or in a microwave oven on high power. Stir chocolate every 30 seconds until melted.
- Dip top of each cooled shortbread cookie into melted chocolate, then into chopped pecans. Place cookies on wax paper and refrigerate to set.

Floating Heaven

BUTTER COOKIES
1 stick (½ cup) unsalted butter, softened
⅔ cup granulated sugar
2 large eggs
1 teaspoon vanilla extract
1 cup plus 2 tablespoons all-purpose flour

DARK CHOCOLATE MOUSSE
5 ounces semisweet chocolate, finely chopped
1 cup plus 2 tablespoons heavy cream

1 tablespoon confectioners' sugar
½ teaspoon vanilla extract

CARAMEL CRÈME ANGLAISE
¾ cup granulated sugar
¼ cup water
2½ cups light cream, scalded
4 large egg yolks
1 stick (½ cup) unsalted butter, softened
2 teaspoons vanilla extract
Unsweetened cocoa powder, for garnish

Yield: About 12 servings

- MAKE THE COOKIES: In a medium bowl, cream the butter and sugar. Beat in the eggs and vanilla. Blend in the flour. Chill the dough for 1 hour.
- Preheat the oven to 325°F. Roll the dough into 24 balls and place 2 inches apart on ungreased cookie sheets. Flatten the cookies with the bottom of a glass and bake for 14 to 16 minutes, or until the edges turn golden. Transfer to racks to cool.
- MEANWHILE, MAKE THE MOUSSE: Place the chocolate in a medium bowl. In a small heavy saucepan, bring ½ cup of the cream to a boil. Pour the hot cream over the chocolate and let stand, covered, for 5 minutes, then stir until smooth. Transfer the chocolate cream to a medium bowl.
- In another medium bowl, beat the remaining ½ cup plus 2 tablespoons cream with the confectioners' sugar and vanilla until soft peaks form. Fold ⅓ of the whipped cream into the chocolate cream to lighten it. Gently but thoroughly fold in the remaining whipped cream. Refrigerate until firm.
- MAKE THE CRÈME ANGLAISE: In a heavy medium saucepan, dissolve the granulated sugar in the water over low heat, stirring constantly. Increase the heat to medium-high and boil without stirring until the syrup turns a deep amber. Remove the pan from the heat and stir in the hot cream (be careful, it will bubble rapidly). Stir until smooth.
- In a small bowl, whisk the egg yolks. Slowly beat in 1 cup of the hot caramel sauce to warm the egg yolks. Transfer the warmed egg yolks to the pan and cook over medium heat, stirring constantly, until the crème anglaise thickens and lightly coats the back of a spoon. Do not boil. Strain the sauce through a fine-mesh sieve and stir in the butter and vanilla. Keep warm.
- ASSEMBLE: With a pastry bag fitted with a star tip, pipe rosettes of mousse over a cookie and top with a second cookie; decorate the top with cocoa powder dusted through a heart-shaped stencil. Spoon ¼ cup of the warm crème anglaise onto a small plate and place a floating heaven on top.

Chocolate-Glazed Shortbread Cookies

<u>SHORTBREAD</u>
3 sticks (1½ cups) salted butter, softened
1 cup confectioners' sugar
1 tablespoon vanilla extract
3 cups all-purpose flour

<u>CHOCOLATE GLAZE</u>
¼ cup heavy cream
6 ounces semisweet chocolate chips
(about 1 cup)
2 teaspoons light corn syrup

Yield: About 4 dozen

- Preheat oven to 325°F.
- Blend butter until smooth in a large bowl using an electric mixer set at medium speed. Slowly blend in the confectioners' sugar. Scrape down the sides of the bowl, then add vanilla extract and combine thoroughly. Add flour and mix at low speed until well blended.
- Divide dough into 2 roughly equal pieces. Flatten each piece into a disk and wrap in plastic wrap. Refrigerate disks until firm, about 1½ hours.
- On a floured board using a floured rolling pin, roll out disks to ⅛-inch thickness. Turn dough often to prevent sticking. Cut cookies with flour-dipped cookie cutters. Bake on ungreased

cookie sheets for 16 to 18 minutes, being careful not to let the cookies brown. Transfer cookies at once to a cool, flat surface with a spatula.
- PREPARE THE CHOCOLATE GLAZE: Heat cream in a small saucepan until scalded; remove from heat. Stir in chocolate chips and corn syrup, cover, and let stand for 15 minutes. With small wire whisk or wooden spoon gently mix glaze until smooth, being careful not to create bubbles in the chocolate. Dip all or half of each cookie into glaze and transfer to a tray or cool cookie sheet covered with wax paper. Chill cookies in refrigerator for 10 minutes to set.

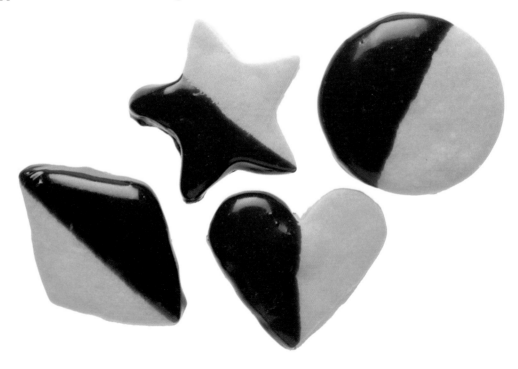

Bizcochitos

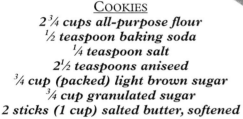

<u>COOKIES</u>
2¾ *cups all-purpose flour*
½ *teaspoon baking soda*
¼ *teaspoon salt*
2½ *teaspoons aniseed*
¾ *cup (packed) light brown sugar*
¾ *cup granulated sugar*
2 *sticks (1 cup) salted butter, softened*

2 *large eggs*
2 *teaspoons brandy*

<u>TOPPING</u>
¼ *cup granulated sugar*
2 *tablespoons ground cinnamon*

Yield: About 3 dozen

- Preheat oven to 300°F.
- Combine flour, baking soda, salt, and aniseed in a small bowl and set aside.
- Blend sugars in a medium bowl using an electric mixer set at medium speed. Add butter and mix until grainy, scraping down the sides of the bowl. Add eggs and brandy, and beat at medium speed until light and fluffy.
- Add the flour mixture and mix at low speed until just combined. Do not overmix.
- Roll rounded tablespoons of dough into 1-inch-diameter balls and then flatten each one slightly with the bottom of a glass or a spatula. Press tops into sugar-cinnamon mixture, then place them on ungreased cookie sheets, 1½ inches apart. Bake 22 to 24 minutes until cookies are slightly brown along edges.
- Transfer cookies immediately to a cool surface with a spatula.

Cinnamon Sugar Butter Cookies

TOPPING
3 tablespoons granulated sugar
1 tablespoon ground cinnamon

COOKIES
2½ cups all-purpose flour
½ teaspoon baking soda
¼ teaspoon salt

1 cup (packed) dark brown sugar
½ cup granulated sugar
2 sticks (1 cup) salted butter, softened
2 large eggs
2 teaspoons vanilla extract

Yield: About 3 dozen

- Preheat oven to 300°F.
- In a small bowl, combine sugar and cinnamon for topping. Set aside.
- In a medium bowl, combine flour, soda, and salt. Mix well with a wire whisk and set aside.
- In a large bowl blend sugars with an electric mixer set at medium speed. Add the butter and mix to form a grainy paste. Scrape sides of bowl, then add the eggs and vanilla. Mix at medium speed until light and fluffy.

- Add the flour mixture and blend at low speed just until combined. Do not overmix. Shape dough into 1-inch balls and roll each ball in cinnamon-sugar topping.
- Place onto ungreased cookie sheets, 2 inches apart. Bake for 18 to 20 minutes. Immediately transfer cookies with a spatula to a cool, flat surface.

Gingersnaps

2½ cups all-purpose flour
½ teaspoon baking soda
¼ teaspoon salt
2 teaspoons ground ginger
1 teaspoon diced crystallized ginger
½ teaspoon allspice
½ teaspoon ground black pepper

1¼ cups (packed) dark brown sugar
1½ sticks (¾ cup) salted butter, softened
1 large egg
¼ cup unsulfurized molasses

Yield: About 2½ dozen

- Preheat oven to 300°F.
- In a medium bowl, combine flour, soda, salt, ground ginger, crystallized ginger, allspice, and pepper. Mix well with a wire whisk. Set aside.
- In a large bowl, mix sugar and butter with an electric mixer set at medium speed. Scrape down the sides of the bowl. Add egg and molasses, and beat at medium speed until light and fluffy.
- Add the flour mixture and mix at low speed just until combined. Do not overmix. Chill the dough in the refrigerator for 1 hour—the dough will be less sticky and easier to handle.
- Form dough into balls 1 inch in diameter. Place onto ungreased cookie sheets, 1½ inches apart. Bake 24 to 25 minutes. Use a spatula to immediately transfer cookies to a cool, flat surface.

Apple Cobbler Cookies

COOKIES
3 cups all-purpose flour
1 teaspoon baking powder
1 teaspoon ground cinnamon
$\frac{1}{2}$ cup granulated sugar
$\frac{1}{2}$ cup (packed) light brown sugar
2 sticks (1 cup) salted butter, softened
2 large eggs
2 teaspoons vanilla extract
$\frac{1}{4}$ cup apple juice
$\frac{1}{2}$ cup apple butter
1 cup tart apples, peeled and chopped

6 ounces raisins (about 1 cup)
4 ounces pecans, finely chopped
(about 1 cup)

CRUMB COATING
$1\frac{1}{4}$ cups (packed) light brown sugar
$1\frac{1}{2}$ cups quick oats (not instant)
$1\frac{1}{4}$ teaspoons ground cinnamon
9 tablespoons salted butter, melted

Yield: About 4 dozen

- Preheat oven to 300°F.
- In medium bowl, combine flour, baking powder, and cinnamon. Mix well with wire whisk. Set aside.
- Combine sugars in a large bowl. Add butter and mix using an electric mixer set at medium speed, scraping down the sides of the bowl. Add eggs and vanilla, and blend until smooth. Thoroughly incorporate the apple juice and apple butter. Add the flour mixture, chopped apples, raisins, and pecans, and blend at low speed until just combined. Do not overmix.
- PREPARE THE CRUMB COATING: Combine sugar, oats, and cinnamon in medium bowl. Mix well with a wire whisk. Add melted butter and mix until dry ingredients are well moistened. Set aside.

- Roll dough into 1-inch-diameter balls. Roll each ball in crumb mixture until well coated. Place cookies on ungreased cookie sheets, 2 inches apart. Bake 24 to 26 minutes, or until cookie is firm to the touch and crumb coating begins to brown. Transfer to a cool, flat surface.

Roll each ball of dough in the crumb coating until it is completely covered. It may be necessary to press the mixture into the dough to make sure it sticks. Place the coated balls on ungreased cookie sheets and bake as directed.

Russian Tea Cakes

COOKIES
2 sticks (1 cup) salted butter, softened
½ cup confectioners' sugar
2 teaspoons vanilla extract
2 cups all-purpose flour
¼ teaspoon salt

TOPPING
½ cup fruit preserves or
2 ounces chopped walnuts (about ½ cup)
¼ cup confectioners' sugar

Yield: About 2 dozen

- Preheat oven to 325°F.
- In a large bowl, cream butter and sugar using an electric mixer. Add vanilla, scraping down sides of bowl as needed. Blend in flour and salt, mixing until thoroughly combined.
- Roll tablespoons of dough into small balls about 1 inch in diameter. Place dough balls on lightly greased cookie sheets about 1 inch apart. Press down the center of each ball with a spoon, forming a depression. Fill each with a teaspoon of preserves or nuts.
- Bake 15 to 20 minutes or until golden brown. Transfer cookies immediately to a cool, flat surface. When cookies are completely cool, dust them lightly with confectioners' sugar.

Brown Buttercrunch Cookies

<u>COOKIES</u>
1 stick (1/2 cup) salted butter, softened
1/2 cup corn syrup
2/3 cup (packed) dark brown sugar
1 cup old-fashioned oats (not quick or instant)
3/4 cup all-purpose flour
1 teaspoon vanilla extract

<u>CHOCOLATE GLAZE</u>
1/4 cup heavy cream
6 ounces semisweet chocolate chips (about 1 cup)
2 teaspoons light corn syrup

Yield: About 2 1/2 dozen

- Preheat oven to 375°F. Line cookie sheets with parchment paper.
- In a medium saucepan, melt butter, corn syrup, and brown sugar over moderate heat, stirring constantly until sugar dissolves. Increase heat to high. When mixture boils remove from heat and stir in oats, flour, and vanilla.
- Bake cookies 1 pan at a time and be ready to work fast. Drop by half teaspoons 3 inches apart onto paper-lined cookie sheets. Bake for 8 minutes or until mixture spreads, bubbles,

and begins to brown. Let cookies cool for 1 to 2 minutes before rolling.
- Roll widest edge of cookie around a pencil or wooden spoon handle, creating a tube. Repeat with remaining cookies. If cookies become too brittle to roll, return to oven for about 30 seconds to soften. Cool rolled cookies completely.
- MAKE THE CHOCOLATE GLAZE: Heat cream in a small saucepan until scalded. Remove from heat and stir in chocolate chips and corn syrup. Cover and let stand about 15 minutes until chocolate has melted. Using a wire whisk or wooden spoon, gently mix glaze until smooth, being careful not to create bubbles.
- When cookies are cool, dip all or half of each cookie into the glaze and return to parchment paper. Refrigerate for 10 to 15 minutes to set.

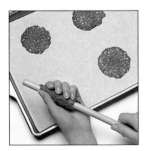

Wrap the warm cookie around a wooden spoon handle (far left). If cookie cools too much, it may crack when rolled. Dip half of each rolled cookie in melted chocolate and return to cookie sheet (left).

Sweetie Pies

2 ounces unsweetened chocolate
4 ounces semisweet chocolate chips
(about ¾ cup)
1 stick (½ cup) salted butter, softened
1 cup granulated sugar
2 large eggs
2 teaspoons vanilla extract
1½ cups all-purpose flour

6 ounces semisweet chocolate chips
(about 1 cup)
3 ounces white chocolate chips
(about ½ cup)
1½ ounces milk chocolate chips
(about ¼ cup)

Yield: About 2½ dozen

- Preheat oven to 375°F. Line cookie sheets with wax paper.
- In a double boiler, melt the unsweetened chocolate and the first batch of chocolate chips. Stir frequently with wooden spoon or wire whisk until creamy and smooth.
- Pour melted chocolate into a large bowl. Add butter and beat with electric mixer at medium speed until thoroughly combined.
- Add the sugar, eggs, and vanilla. Beat on medium speed until well blended. Scrape down sides of bowl.

- Add the flour and the 3 types of chocolate chips. Mix at low speed just until combined. Chips should be distributed equally throughout the dough.
- Roll a heaping tablespoon of dough into a ball, about 1½ inches in diameter. Place dough balls onto paper-lined pans, 2 inches apart. With the palm of your hand, flatten each ball to ½-inch thickness.
- Bake for 10 to 12 minutes. Transfer cookies with a spatula to a cool, flat surface.

Choconut Macaroons

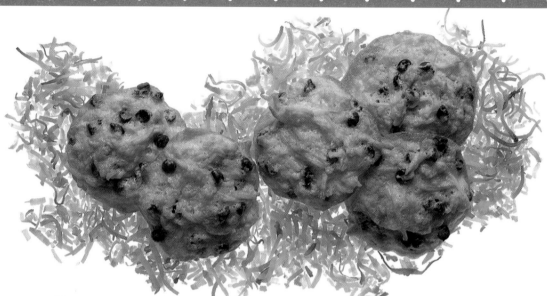

¼ *cup granulated sugar*
2 tablespoons almond paste (marzipan)
1 cup shredded sweetened coconut
2 ounces mini semisweet chocolate chips
(about ⅓ cup)

3 large egg whites
½ *teaspoon cream of tartar*

Yield: About 1½ dozen

- Preheat oven to 325°F.
- Combine almond paste and sugar in a medium bowl. Using your fingers, work paste into sugar completely. Add coconut and chocolate chips and stir to combine.
- In another medium bowl, beat egg whites until fluffy using absolutely clean beaters. Add cream of tartar and beat on high until stiff peaks form. Add half of beaten egg whites to

coconut mixture and combine to lighten. Fold in remaining whites gently, being careful not to deflate.
- Drop by rounded teaspoons onto lightly greased cookie sheets. Bake 20 minutes, or until tops are lightly browned. Cool 1 minute on the cookie sheets before transferring cookies to a cool surface.

Spoon about half of the beaten egg whites into the cookie batter, and stir lightly but thoroughly until the egg whites are well combined (far left). Add the remaining egg whites and, using a spatula, bring the lightened batter up from the bottom of the bowl over the egg whites (left). Continue folding the egg whites into the batter just until they are incorporated. Be careful not to deflate the egg whites.

Cinnamon Maple Rings

PASTRY
2 cups all-purpose flour
¼ cup granulated sugar
2 sticks (1 cup) salted butter, chilled &
sliced into 8 pieces
¼ cup pure maple syrup, chilled
2 to 4 tablespoons ice water

FILLING
¼ cup granulated sugar
4 teaspoons ground cinnamon

TOPPING
¼ cup pure maple syrup

Yield: About 4 dozen

- Combine flour and sugar in a medium bowl using an electric mixer set on medium speed. Add butter and mix until the dough forms pea-size pellets. Add chilled maple syrup and 2 tablespoons of water, and mix on low speed until dough can be formed into a ball. Do not overmix, or the pastry will be tough.
- Separate dough into 2 balls and flatten into disks. Wrap dough tightly in plastic wrap or place in plastic bags. Refrigerate for 2 hours or until firm.
- PREPARE THE FILLING: Combine sugar and cinnamon in a small bowl. Preheat oven to 325°F.
- Using a floured rolling pin on a floured board, roll one piece of dough into a rough rectangle 10 inches wide, 15 inches long, and ⅛ inch thick. Sprinkle dough with half of cinnamon-sugar filling. Starting with smaller side, roll

After sprinkling the dough with sugar and cinnamon, roll the dough into a tight cylinder (right). Just before sliding the cookies into the oven, brush the tops with maple syrup (far right).

dough up tightly into a cylinder. Dampen edge with water and seal. Repeat with remaining dough. Wrap each roll in plastic wrap and refrigerate for 1 hour.
- Using a sharp thin knife, cut ¼-inch slices from each roll. Place slices on ungreased baking sheets, 1 inch apart. Brush tops lightly with ¼ cup maple syrup. Bake for 16 to 17 minutes, or until light golden brown. Immediately transfer cookies to a cool, flat surface with a spatula.

Party Time Cookies

1½ sticks (¾ cup) salted butter, softened
⅓ cup granulated sugar
1 teaspoon vanilla extract
¼ teaspoon almond extract
1 cup all-purpose flour

6 ounces semisweet chocolate chips
(about 1 cup)
4 ounces slivered almonds (about 1 cup)

Yield: About 2 dozen

- Preheat oven to 350°F.
- Cream butter and sugar together in a medium bowl using an electric mixer set at medium speed. Add extracts and beat well. Scrape bowl. Add flour, chocolate chips, and almonds, and blend on low speed until just combined. Do not overmix.
- Shape rounded tablespoons into 1½-inch balls and place on ungreased baking sheets, 2 inches apart. Press balls with palm of hand or bottom of drinking glass into ½-inch-thick rounds.
- Bake 15 to 17 minutes or until cookies just begin to brown. Transfer cookies to a cool, flat surface.

Snowy White Chocolate Crescents

1½ cups all-purpose flour
⅓ cup cocoa powder, unsweetened
1 stick (½ cup) salted butter, softened
1 cup granulated sugar
1 teaspoon vanilla extract

1 large egg
½ cup confectioners' sugar

Yield: About 2½ dozen

- Preheat oven to 325°F.
- In a small bowl, combine flour and cocoa. Mix well with a wire whisk and set aside.
- In a medium bowl, cream butter and sugar with an electric mixer on medium speed. Add vanilla and egg, and beat until light and smooth. Scrape down sides of bowl, then add flour and cocoa mixture. Blend on low speed until fully incorporated. The dough will be dry and crumbly.

- Shape a level tablespoon of dough into a 3½-inch log. Slightly bend the log to form a crescent shape. Form remaining dough into crescents, and place on ungreased baking sheets, 1 inch apart. Bake 15 to 17 minutes or until the outside of cookie is hard but the center remains soft.
- Cool on pan for 2 to 3 minutes, then transfer to a flat surface to cool a few minutes more. While still warm, roll the cookies in confectioners' sugar until coated.

To form the chocolate cookies, roll dough briskly between your hands into 3½-inch logs (far left). Then bend each log slightly to form a crescent shape (left) and bake.

Double-Dipped Chocolate Shortbread Cookies

COOKIES

3 ounces semisweet chocolate, finely chopped
1½ sticks (¾ cup) unsalted butter, softened
1 teaspoon vanilla extract
1½ cups all-purpose flour
½ cup confectioners' sugar
2 teaspoons unsweetened cocoa powder
⅛ teaspoon salt

FOR DIPPING

4 ounces white chocolate, finely chopped
½ cup heavy cream
3 ounces semisweet chocolate, finely chopped

Yield: About 2½ dozen

- MAKE THE COOKIES: In a double boiler, melt the semisweet chocolate over hot, not simmering, water. Set aside to cool to lukewarm.
- In a large bowl with an electric mixer, cream the butter. Beat in the melted chocolate. Then beat in the vanilla, flour, sugar, cocoa, and salt. Wrap and chill the dough for 30 minutes, or until firm enough to roll into balls.
- Preheat the oven to 350°F. Roll the dough into 1-inch balls, then roll each ball into a thick log. Place on an ungreased cookie sheet and press the dough to a ¼-inch thickness with the tines of a fork, keeping the cookies oval in shape.
- Bake the cookies for 8 to 10 minutes, or until

just set; do not overbake. Transfer to wire racks to cool completely.
- DIP THE COOKIES: In a small bowl set over a saucepan of hot water, melt the white chocolate with ¼ cup of the cream; stir until smooth. Keep the mixture over the hot water so it will be liquid for dipping. In another small bowl set over a saucepan of hot water, melt the semisweet chocolate with the remaining ¼ cup cream; stir until smooth. Keep warm.
- Dip one end of a cookie in the white chocolate and the other end in the dark chocolate and return to the cooling racks so the chocolate can set. Repeat with the remaining cookies.

Bar Cookies

Chocolate Chip Butterscotch Bars

2 cups all-purpose flour
½ teaspoon baking soda
1 cup (packed) dark brown sugar
2 sticks (1 cup) salted butter, softened
1 large egg
2 teaspoons vanilla extract

4 ounces chopped pecans (about 1 cup)
9 ounces semisweet chocolate chips
(about 1½ cups)

Yield: 16 bars

- Preheat oven to 300°F. Grease an 8-by-8-inch baking pan.
- Combine flour and soda in a medium bowl. Mix well with a wire whisk. Set aside.
- In a large bowl, use an electric mixer to blend the sugar and butter. Add egg and vanilla, and beat at medium speed until light and smooth. Scrape down the sides of the bowl, then add the flour mixture, pecans, and chocolate chips.

Blend at low speed until just combined. Do not overmix.
- Transfer batter into the prepared pan, and level top with a rubber spatula. Bake in center of oven for 35 to 45 minutes or until toothpick comes out clean but center is still soft. Cool on rack to room temperature. Cut with sharp knife into 1-by-2-inch bars.

Peanut Butter & Jelly Squares

2½ cups all-purpose flour
½ teaspoon baking powder
2 sticks (1 cup) salted butter, softened
1 cup granulated sugar
1 large egg
2 teaspoons vanilla extract

½ cup jam or jelly
¼ cup creamy peanut butter
2 tablespoons confectioners' sugar

Yield: 24 squares

- Preheat oven to 325°F. Lightly grease a 9-by-13-inch baking pan.
- In a medium bowl, combine flour and baking powder. Mix well with a wire whisk and set aside.
- In another medium bowl with an electric mixer on medium speed, combine butter and sugar to form a grainy paste. Add egg and vanilla, and mix until smooth. Scrape down sides of bowl. Then add flour mixture and blend at low speed until thoroughly combined. Dough will be firm.
- Divide dough into 2 pieces; form disks and wrap tightly in plastic wrap or a plastic bag. Refrigerate 1 hour.
- On floured board using a floured rolling pin, roll out each disk to 9 by 13 inches, about ¼ inch thick. Place 1 piece in bottom and up the sides of prepared baking pan. Refrigerate 10 minutes more.
- Spread half the jelly on dough. Layer peanut butter on top of jelly, then top with remaining jelly. Sprinkle with confectioners' sugar. Place second dough rectangle on top of peanut-butter-and-jelly layer. Pinch down side edges all around inside of pan.
- Bake 35 to 40 minutes or until golden brown and firm to the touch in the center. Cool in pan, then cut into squares.

Golden White-Chunk Nutty Bars

2 cups all-purpose flour
$\frac{1}{2}$ teaspoon baking soda
$\frac{1}{4}$ teaspoon salt
$1\frac{1}{2}$ sticks ($\frac{3}{4}$ cup) unsalted butter, cut into
tablespoons
1 cup (packed) dark brown sugar
2 medium eggs

$\frac{1}{2}$ cup shredded coconut
2 teaspoons vanilla extract
10 ounces white chocolate, coarsely
chopped
1 cup coarsely chopped pecans

Yield: 16 bars

- Preheat the oven to 300°F. Grease a 9-by-13-inch baking pan.
- In a medium bowl, combine the flour, baking soda, and salt.
- In another medium bowl with an electric mixer, cream the butter and sugar. Beat in the eggs, coconut, and vanilla, then blend slowly until smooth. Add the flour mixture, chopped chocolate, and pecans.

- Scrape the dough into the prepared baking pan and level and smooth the surface. Bake for 40 to 45 minutes, or until the center is set and the top is golden.
- Place the pan on a wire rack to cool to room temperature before cutting into 16 bars.

Cherry Cream Bars

BROWNIE LAYER
1 cup all-purpose flour
1 cup granulated sugar
¾ cup (packed) dark brown sugar
½ teaspoon salt
4 ounces unsweetened chocolate
1½ sticks (¾ cup) unsalted butter, softened
4 large eggs
¼ cup milk
2½ teaspoons vanilla extract
1 cup coarsely chopped walnuts
1 cup drained canned Bing cherries (½ cup of the syrup reserved)
1 cup semisweet chocolate chips

CHOCOLATE-CHERRY GLAZE
3 ounces semisweet chocolate, chopped
½ cup syrup reserved from cherries
¼ cup heavy cream
2 teaspoons kirsch (cherry brandy)
2 teaspoons granulated sugar

CHERRY CREAM
1 cup heavy cream
3 tablespoons confectioners' sugar
1 tablespoon kirsch (cherry brandy)
½ cup chopped drained canned Bing cherries

Yield: 12 bars

- Preheat the oven to 300°F. Grease a 7-by-11-inch baking pan.
- MAKE THE BROWNIE LAYER: In a large bowl, whisk together the flour, granulated sugar, brown sugar, and salt.
- In a double boiler, melt the unsweetened chocolate and butter together over low heat, stirring until smooth.
- In a small bowl, lightly beat the eggs with the milk and vanilla.
- Add the chocolate mixture and beaten eggs to the dry ingredients and stir to blend. Stir in the walnuts, cherries, and chocolate chips.
- Pour the batter into the prepared pan and bake for 1 hour and 10 minutes, or until a cake tester inserted in the center comes out with a few crumbs clinging to it. Cool the brownies in the pan on a rack.
- MEANWHILE, MAKE THE CHOCOLATE-CHERRY GLAZE: Place the semisweet chocolate in a medium bowl.
- In a small saucepan, bring the reserved cherry syrup to a boil. Simmer until reduced by half. Add the cream and bring to a boil. Remove from the heat and stir in the kirsch and granulated sugar.

- Pour the hot cream mixture over the chocolate. Let stand, covered, for 5 minutes, then stir until smooth. Set aside to cool to room temperature, then pour the glaze over the cooled brownies.
- MAKE THE CHERRY CREAM: In a medium bowl, beat the cream with the confectioners' sugar and kirsch until stiff peaks form. Fold in the drained chopped cherries.
- Cut into 12 bars and serve with a spoonful of the cherry cream on top.

Bull's Eyes

BLUE-RIBBON CHOCOLATE CHIP COOKIES

$2\frac{1}{2}$ cups all-purpose flour
$\frac{1}{2}$ teaspoon baking soda
$\frac{1}{4}$ teaspoon salt
1 cup (packed) dark brown sugar
$\frac{1}{2}$ cup granulated sugar
2 sticks (1 cup) salted butter, softened
2 large eggs
2 teaspoons vanilla extract
12 ounces semisweet chocolate chips
(about 2 cups)
1 cup sweetened, shredded coconut

DOUBLE-RICH CHOCOLATE COOKIES

$1\frac{1}{4}$ cups all-purpose flour
$\frac{1}{4}$ teaspoon baking soda
$\frac{1}{8}$ teaspoon salt
$\frac{1}{4}$ cup unsweetened cocoa powder
$\frac{1}{2}$ cup (packed) dark brown sugar
$\frac{1}{4}$ cup plus 2 tablespoons granulated sugar
1 stick ($\frac{1}{2}$ cup) salted butter, softened
1 large egg
1 large egg yolk
1 teaspoon vanilla extract
6 ounces semisweet chocolate chips
(about 1 cup)

Yield: 24 bars

- Preheat oven to 300°F and grease a 9-by-13-inch glass baking dish.
- FIRST, MAKE THE BLUE-RIBBON COOKIES: In a medium bowl combine flour, soda, and salt. Mix well with a wire whisk.
- In a large bowl, blend sugars and butter with an electric mixer. Scrape sides of bowl, then add eggs and vanilla extract. Beat at medium speed until light and fluffy. Add flour mixture and chocolate chips, and mix just until combined. Press dough evenly into prepared pan and sprinkle with coconut. Set aside.
- NEXT, MAKE THE DOUBLE-RICH COOKIES: In a medium bowl combine flour, soda, salt, and cocoa powder with a wire whisk.
- In a large bowl, blend sugars and butter with mixer at medium speed. Scrape bowl, then add eggs and vanilla, and beat until well combined. Add the flour mixture and chocolate chips, and blend on low. Do not overmix.
- Drop the Double-Rich dough by rounded teaspoons onto the Blue-Ribbon dough. Evenly space the darker dough on top of the lighter dough to resemble bull's eyes. Bake 50 to 60 minutes, until a toothpick inserted in center comes out clean. Cool and cut.

Creamy Layered Pudding Bars

CRUST
1 stick (¹⁄₂ cup) salted butter, softened
¹⁄₄ cup granulated sugar
1 large egg yolk
1 teaspoon vanilla extract
1 cup cake flour
¹⁄₈ teaspoon salt

FILLING
¹⁄₂ cup granulated sugar
1 tablespoon cornstarch
5 large egg yolks
1 teaspoon vanilla extract
1 cup whipping cream
6 ounces mini semisweet chocolate chips
(about 1 cup)
4 ounces pecans, chopped (about 1 cup)

Yield: 16 bars

- Preheat oven to 325°F. Grease an 8-inch square baking pan.
- In a medium bowl, cream the butter and sugar with an electric mixer at medium speed, scraping down the sides of the bowl. Add single egg yolk and vanilla and beat at medium speed until light and fluffy. Add the flour and the salt, and blend at low speed until just combined.
- Turn dough out into prepared pan, and place in refrigerator for 15 minutes. When dough is chilled, lightly flour your hands and press the dough to ¹⁄₄-inch thickness on bottom and sides of pan. Dough should extend 1 inch up sides of pan. Return pan to refrigerator while you prepare the filling.
- PREPARE THE FILLING: Combine sugar and cornstarch in a small bowl. Mix well with a wire whisk. Set aside.
- In a medium bowl with an electric mixer set on medium-high speed, beat the 5 egg yolks 5 minutes or until they are light and fluffy. Add cornstarch-sugar mixture and mix on medium until combined. Add the vanilla, whipping cream, chocolate chips, and pecans and blend at low speed—scraping bowl as needed—until thoroughly combined. Pour filling into pastry-lined pan.
- Bake 55 to 60 minutes or until filling is set and golden brown. Chill 4 hours or overnight. Cut into 16 bars.

Press the chilled dough firmly into the bottom of a greased 8-by-8-inch pan. The dough should extend up the sides of the pan by about an inch. Lightly flour your hands before you begin to prevent the dough from sticking to them.

Pecan Pie Bars

PASTRY
1½ cups all-purpose flour
1 stick (½ cup) salted butter, chilled
5 to 6 tablespoons ice water

FILLING
5 tablespoons salted butter
1 cup (packed) dark brown sugar

½ cup light corn syrup
2 teaspoons vanilla extract
3 large eggs, beaten
6 ounces chopped pecans (about 1½ cups)
16 pecan halves

Yield: 16 squares

- Preheat oven to 350°F.
- In a medium bowl, combine flour and chilled butter with a pastry cutter until dough resembles coarse meal. Add water gradually and mix just until dough holds together and can be shaped into a ball. Or, use a food processor fitted with metal blade to combine flour and butter until they resemble coarse meal. Add water by tablespoonfuls and process just until a dough ball begins to form. Wrap dough tightly in plastic wrap or a plastic bag. Refrigerate 1 hour or until firm.
- On floured board using a floured rolling pin, roll out dough into a 10-inch square. Fold dough in half and then into quarters. Place it in an 8-by-8-inch baking pan. Unfold the dough and press it into the corners and up along the sides of the pan. Refrigerate for 15 minutes.
- PREPARE THE FILLING: Melt 5 tablespoons of butter in medium saucepan over medium heat. Remove from heat, and stir in sugar and corn syrup. Mix until smooth. Add vanilla and eggs, and beat with spoon until thoroughly combined. Fold in chopped pecans.
- Pour the pecan filling into the pastry-lined pan. If dough extends beyond filling mixture trim dough with a knife. Place pan in center of oven and bake 50 to 60 minutes or until filling is set. Cool on wire rack. Cut into 2-inch squares, and top each with a pecan half. Serve at room temperature or chilled.

To transfer the dough from the work surface to the pan, first fold it into quarters. Place the dough in the baking pan (far left), then unfold it. Press the dough into the bottom, corners, and up the sides of the pan (left). Refrigerate for 15 minutes while you prepare the filling.

Kandy Fun Kakes

4 tablespoons (¼ cup) unsalted butter
4 cups mini marshmallows
2 teaspoons vanilla extract
4 cups crisp rice cereal
¾ cup butterscotch caramel fudge topping

12 ounces milk chocolate,
coarsely chopped

Yield: 16 squares

- Lightly grease a 7-by-11-inch or an 8-inch square baking pan.
- In a large saucepan, melt the butter over low heat. Add the marshmallows and stir until blended. Remove from the heat and stir in the vanilla.
- Stir in the cereal and mix with a wooden spoon until thoroughly blended. Scrape the mixture into the prepared pan. With lightly buttered hands or a lightly buttered spatula, press gently on the mixture to level. Place in the freezer for 10 minutes.

- In a small saucepan, warm the butterscotch caramel fudge topping to lukewarm (do not let it get hot). Remove from the heat and set aside to cool slightly.
- Pour the warm butterscotch topping over the cereal layer, spreading evenly. Place in the freezer for 10 minutes.
- In a double boiler, melt the chocolate over hot, not simmering, water. Set aside to cool slightly. Spread the chocolate on top of the caramel mixture. Chill to set the chocolate. Cut into squares and serve.

Granola Date Bars

FILLING
8 ounces chopped dates (about 1½ cups)
½ cup shredded sweetened coconut
¾ cup half-and-half or light cream
1 teaspoon vanilla extract

GRANOLA BASE
2 cups quick oats (not instant)
¾ cup all-purpose flour
1 cup (packed) dark brown sugar
½ teaspoon baking soda
½ teaspoon ground cinnamon
1 stick (½ cup) salted butter, melted

Yield: 16 squares

- PREPARE THE FILLING: Heat dates, coconut, and half-and-half in medium saucepan over medium heat. Stir occasionally until mixture boils and thickens, about 15 minutes. Remove from heat and stir in vanilla. Set aside to cool.
- PREPARE THE GRANOLA BASE: Combine oats, flour, sugar, soda, and cinnamon in medium bowl. Mix well with wire whisk. Pour melted butter over dry ingredients and stir with large wooden spoon until thoroughly moistened.

- Press about 3 cups of the granola mixture into bottom of an 8-by-8-inch baking pan. Place in refrigerator about 30 minutes to harden.
- Preheat oven to 350°F.
- Spread the cooled date filling evenly over granola base. Sprinkle the remaining granola mixture (about ¾ cup) over the date filling. Bake for 25 to 30 minutes or until the granola topping is slightly browned and crisp. Cool to room temperature before cutting into 2-inch squares.

After the dates, coconut, and half-and-half have come to a boil continue to cook the mixture until it has thickened. Stir occasionally to prevent sticking.

Triple-Layered Lemon Bars

CRUST
1 stick ($\frac{1}{2}$ cup) salted butter, softened
$\frac{1}{4}$ cup confectioners' sugar
1 teaspoon vanilla extract
1 cup all-purpose flour

CREAM CHEESE FILLING
8 ounces cream cheese, softened
$1\frac{1}{2}$ cups confectioners' sugar
1 large egg
1 teaspoon lemon extract

LEMON CURD
4 large egg yolks
1 tablespoon cornstarch
$\frac{3}{4}$ cup granulated sugar
$\frac{3}{4}$ cup water
2 medium lemons grated for 2 teaspoons lemon peel, and squeezed for $\frac{1}{4}$ cup fresh lemon juice
2 tablespoons salted butter, softened

TOPPING
2 tablespoons confectioners' sugar

Yield: 12 bars

- Preheat oven to 325°F.
- PREPARE THE SHORTBREAD CRUST: Cream butter and sugar in medium bowl with electric mixer set on high speed. Add vanilla and mix until combined. Add flour and mix at low speed until fully incorporated. Press dough evenly into bottom of an 8-by-8-inch baking pan. Refrigerate until firm, approximately 30 minutes. Prick shortbread crust with fork and bake for 30 minutes or until crust turns golden brown. Cool on rack to room temperature.
- PREPARE THE CREAM CHEESE FILLING WHILE THE CRUST IS BAKING: Beat cream cheese and sugar until smooth in medium bowl with electric mixer set on high speed. Add egg and lemon extract and beat on medium speed until light and smooth. Cover bowl tightly and refrigerate.
- PREPARE THE LEMON CURD: Blend the egg yolks with the cornstarch and sugar in medium non-aluminum saucepan. Place over low heat and slowly whisk in water and lemon juice. Increase heat to medium-low and cook, stirring constantly, until mixture thickens enough to coat the back of a spoon. Remove from heat. Add lemon peel and butter and cool for 10 minutes.
- ASSEMBLE THE BARS: Spread chilled cream cheese filling evenly over cooled shortbread crust with spatula. Spread lemon curd evenly over cream cheese filling. Place pan in center of oven. Bake 30 to 40 minutes or until edges begin to turn light golden brown. Cool to room temperature on rack. Chill in refrigerator 1 hour before cutting into bars. Dust top with confectioners' sugar.

Check the lemon curd to see if it has reached the desired consistency. If it thickly coats the back of a spoon, it is ready. Add the butter and lemon peel and proceed as directed above.

Super Fudge Brownies

6 ounces unsweetened baking chocolate
2 sticks (1 cup) salted butter, softened
4 large eggs
2 cups granulated sugar
1 tablespoon vanilla extract

$\frac{1}{2}$ cup all-purpose flour
6 ounces semisweet chocolate chips
(about 1 cup)

Yield: 16 brownies, 2 inches square

- Preheat oven to 300°F. Grease an 8-by-8-inch baking pan.
- Combine unsweetened baking chocolate and butter in a medium saucepan. Melt over medium-low heat, stirring constantly until pieces are almost melted. Remove from heat and stir until smooth.
- In a large bowl, using an electric mixer on medium speed, beat eggs until light yellow in color—about 5 minutes. Add sugar and blend on low until thoroughly combined.

- Add vanilla and melted chocolate to the egg and sugar mixture. Blend on low speed until smooth. Add the flour and mix thoroughly.
- Pour batter into greased pan. Smooth surface with a spatula, and sprinkle uniformly with chocolate chips. Bake on the center rack of oven for 45 to 55 minutes. The batter should be set and a toothpick inserted into the center should come out clean. Do not overbake.
- Cool to room temperature. Cover and refrigerate for at least 1 hour. Cut and serve chilled.

Coconut Mud Bars

BOTTOM LAYER
1⅓ cups all-purpose flour
½ teaspoon baking powder
Pinch of salt
½ cup (packed) dark brown sugar
1 stick (½ cup) unsalted butter, slightly softened and cut into small pieces

GANACHE
10 ounces semisweet chocolate, finely chopped
¾ cup heavy cream

TOPPING
4 tablespoons (¼ cup) unsalted butter, softened
½ cup granulated sugar
2 teaspoons vanilla extract
¼ teaspoon coconut extract (optional)
2 large eggs
1½ cups shredded coconut
1½ cups chopped pecans

Yield: 24 bars

- Preheat the oven to 350°F. Lightly grease a 9-by-13-inch baking pan.
- MAKE THE BOTTOM LAYER: In a medium bowl, combine the flour, baking powder, salt, and brown sugar. With a pastry blender, cut the butter into the dry ingredients until the mixture resembles coarse meal. Press the mixture into the bottom of the prepared pan. Bake for 10 minutes, or until the crust is just set. Place the pan on a rack to cool, but leave the oven on.
- MEANWHILE, MAKE THE GANACHE: Place the chocolate in a medium bowl. In a small saucepan, bring the cream to a simmer. Pour the hot cream over the chocolate; let stand for 5 minutes, then stir until smooth. Pour the ganache over the crust and refrigerate for about 15 minutes to set the ganache.

- PREPARE THE TOPPING: In a medium bowl, cream the butter. Add the granulated sugar, vanilla, and coconut extract, if desired, and beat until blended. Beat in the eggs. Stir in the coconut and pecans.
- Drop the coconut-pecan topping evenly over the ganache and spread gently. Bake for 25 to 30 minutes, or until the top is golden brown. Set the pan on a wire rack to cool. Cut into bars.

Melt the chocolate for the ganache by pouring hot cream over the finely chopped chocolate. Let stand for about 5 minutes, then stir until melted and smooth.

Creamy Peanut Butter Chocolate Bars

CRUST
8 medium-size butter or chocolate chip cookies
1 stick (¼ cup) salted butter, melted

CHOCOLATE LAYERS
15 ounces milk chocolate chips (about 2½ cups)

PEANUT BUTTER FILLING
1½ cups creamy peanut butter
1 stick (½ cup) salted butter, softened
3 cups confectioners' sugar
2 teaspoons vanilla extract

Yield: 24 to 36 bars

- Preheat oven to 325°F.
- In food processor or blender, process cookies until finely ground. Add butter and mix together completely. Press crumb mixture into bottom of 8-by-8-inch baking pan and bake 10 minutes. Cool to room temperature.
- Melt chocolate in double boiler over slightly simmering water. Or, microwave the chocolate, stirring every 30 seconds until completely melted. Pour half of the melted chocolate into pan and smooth evenly over crust. Place pan in refrigerator. Keep remaining chocolate warm.
- PREPARE THE PEANUT BUTTER FILLING: Blend peanut butter and butter together until smooth using a food processor or electric mixer. Slowly beat in confectioners' sugar and then add vanilla. Beat until smooth. Spread peanut butter filling over the chilled chocolate layer. Finish by pouring remaining warm chocolate over filling and spreading smooth. Chill in refrigerator 1 hour or until firm. Cut into bars to serve.

Spoon the peanut butter filling over the chilled chocolate and cookie base (far left), then spread smooth. Complete the bar by pouring the melted chocolate over the peanut butter layer (left), spreading it smooth, and chilling in the refrigerator until firm.

Twice-Topped Brownies

BROWNIE LAYER
4 ounces unsweetened chocolate
1 stick (½ cup) salted butter
I cup all-purpose flour
¼ teaspoon salt
2 large eggs
1 cup (packed) light brown sugar
2 teaspoons vanilla extract
½ cup chopped pecans
½ cup mini semisweet chocolate chips

VANILLA CREAM
1 stick (½ cup) salted butter, softened
4 ounces cream cheese, softened
1 teaspoon vanilla extract
1¼ cups confectioners' sugar

CHOCOLATE DRIZZLE
2 ounces semisweet chocolate chips
2 tablespoons heavy cream

Yield: 16 bars

- Preheat the oven to 325°F. Grease a 7-by-11-inch baking pan.
- PREPARE THE BROWNIE LAYER: In a double boiler, melt the unsweetened chocolate and butter together, stirring until smooth. Set aside to cool slightly.
- In a small bowl, combine the flour and salt.
- In a medium bowl, beat the eggs and brown sugar together. Beat in the chocolate mixture and the vanilla. Stir in the flour mixture. Then stir in the pecans and mini chocolate chips.
- Spread the batter in the prepared pan and bake for 22 to 25 minutes, or until a cake tester inserted into the center comes out clean. Cool in the pan on a rack.

- MAKE THE VANILLA CREAM: In a medium bowl, cream the butter and cream cheese until light and fluffy. Gradually beat in the vanilla and confectioners' sugar. Spread the vanilla cream over the cooled brownies. Refrigerate until set.
- PREPARE THE DRIZZLE: In a double boiler, melt the chocolate chips and cream over hot, not simmering, water. Stir until smooth, then set aside to cool slightly. Dip a fork into the melted chocolate mixture and drizzle in a random pattern over the vanilla cream layer.
- Chill until ready to serve.

Vermont Maple Walnut Bars

BARS
2 cups all-purpose flour
½ teaspoon baking soda
½ cup (packed) light brown sugar
1 stick (½ cup) salted butter, softened
1 cup pure maple syrup
1 large egg
2 teaspoons vanilla extract
4 ounces walnuts, chopped (about 1 cup)

MAPLE FROSTING
1 stick (½ cup) salted butter, softened
2 ounces cream cheese, softened
1 tablespoon (packed) light brown sugar
3 tablespoons pure maple syrup
¼ cup plus 2 tablespoons confectioners' sugar
Walnut halves (optional)

Yield: 12 to 16 bars

- Preheat oven to 325°F. Grease an 8-by-8-inch baking pan.
- MAKE BARS: In a medium bowl, combine flour and soda. Mix well with a wire whisk and set aside.
- In a large bowl with an electric mixer, blend sugar and butter to form a grainy paste. Scrape down sides of bowl, then add syrup, egg and vanilla. Beat at medium speed until smooth.
- Add the flour mixture and walnuts, and blend at low speed just until combined. Do not overmix.
- Pour batter into baking pan and smooth top with a spatula. Bake 40 to 45 minutes or until toothpick inserted into center comes out clean. Cool in pan 15 minutes, then invert onto cooling rack. Cool completely before icing.
- MAKE FROSTING: In a medium bowl, cream butter and cream cheese with electric mixer at high speed. Add brown sugar and maple syrup, and beat until smooth. Reduce mixer speed to medium, and slowly add confectioners' sugar. Once sugar is incorporated, increase speed to high, and mix until smooth. If frosting appears thin, gradually add confectioners' sugar until frosting thickens.
- Using a metal spatula, spread frosting on top and sides of maple bars. If desired, make designs on frosting or decorate with walnut halves.

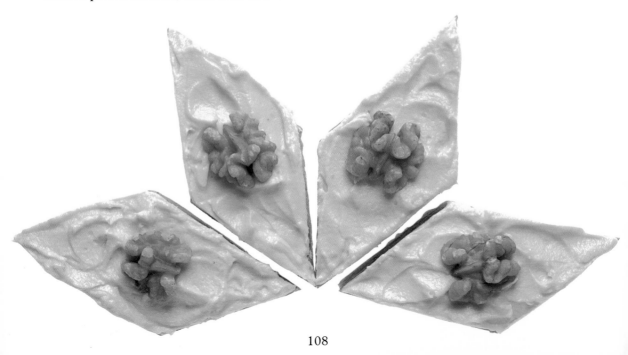

Special Treats

Chocolate Turtle Pie

<u>CRUST</u>
1¼ cups graham cracker crumbs
4 tablespoons (¼ cup) unsalted butter,
melted
2 tablespoons granulated sugar
3 ounces milk chocolate, finely chopped

<u>FILLING</u>
¾ cup granulated sugar
3 tablespoons water

2 cups heavy cream, scalded
5 large egg yolks
6 ounces semisweet chocolate, finely
chopped
1 teaspoon vanilla extract
¼ cup chopped pecans
¼ cup semisweet chocolate chips

Yield: One 9-inch pie

- Preheat the oven to 350°F.
- MAKE THE CRUST: In a medium bowl, blend the graham cracker crumbs, butter, and sugar. Stir in the milk chocolate. Press the crust mixture into the bottom and up the sides of a 9-inch pie plate. Refrigerate until ready to use.
- PREPARE THE FILLING: In a heavy, medium saucepan, dissolve the sugar in the water over low heat, stirring constantly. Bring to a boil over medium-high heat, then let boil without stirring until the syrup turns a light amber. While the syrup is boiling, brush down the sides of the pan from time to time with a wet pastry brush to prevent crystals from forming. Remove the pan from the heat and stir in the hot cream (be careful, it will bubble rapidly).

Continue stirring, over heat if necessary, until all of the caramel is dissolved into the cream.
- In a medium bowl, lightly beat the egg yolks. Whisk about ½ cup of the hot caramel cream into the eggs to warm them. Transfer the warmed eggs to the caramel cream in the saucepan. Stir in the chopped semisweet chocolate and the vanilla, stirring until melted and smooth.
- Pour the filling mixture into the pie crust. Sprinkle the pecans and chocolate chips on top. Bake for about 35 minutes, or until the center is just set. Transfer to a wire rack to cool completely, then refrigerate until firm, about 4 hours.

Milk Chocolate Toffee Cream Pie

CRUST
1½ cups chocolate wafer crumbs
5 tablespoons (¼ cup plus 1 tablespoon)
unsalted butter, melted
2 tablespoons granulated sugar

FILLING
6 ounces milk chocolate, coarsely chopped
¾ cup heavy cream
8 ounces cream cheese, softened
¼ cup (packed) light brown sugar
1 tablespoon vanilla extract
¾ cup chopped chocolate-covered toffee
candy

Yield: One 9-inch pie

- Preheat the oven to 350°F.
- MAKE THE CRUST: In a medium bowl, combine the wafer crumbs, butter, and sugar. Press the mixture into the bottom and up the sides of a 9-inch pie plate. Bake for 10 minutes. Place on a wire rack to cool.
- PREPARE THE FILLING: Place the chocolate in a small bowl. In a small saucepan, bring ½ cup of the cream to a simmer. Pour the hot cream over the chocolate. Let stand, cov-

Use your fingers to shape a layer of the wafer crumb mixture over the bottom and sides of a 9-inch pie plate.

ered, for 5 minutes, then stir until smooth.
- In a medium bowl with an electric mixer, beat the cream cheese, sugar, and vanilla until smooth. Beat in the remaining ¼ cup cream. Gently beat in the cooled chocolate mixture. Fold in ½ cup of the chopped toffee candy.
- Pour the filling into the cooled crust, and sprinkle with the remaining ¼ cup of chopped toffee. Chill until firm, about 2 hours.

Mocha Mousse Cheesecake

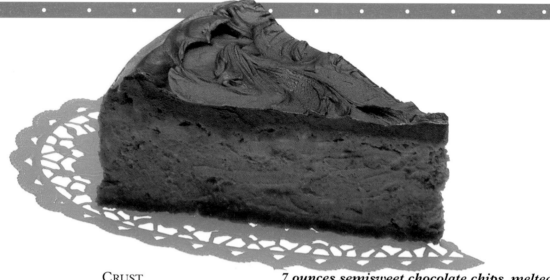

CRUST
**4 ounces chocolate chip cookie crumbs
(about 1 cup)
2 tablespoons salted butter, melted**

FILLING
**24 ounces cream cheese, softened
$\frac{1}{2}$ cup granulated sugar
$\frac{1}{2}$ cup (packed) light brown sugar
8 ounces sour cream (about 1 cup)
3 large eggs**

**7 ounces semisweet chocolate chips, melted
(about 1$\frac{1}{4}$ cups)
$\frac{1}{2}$ cup coffee, freshly brewed
1 tablespoon vanilla extract**

GLAZE
**5 ounces semisweet chocolate
(about $\frac{3}{4}$ cup)
$\frac{1}{2}$ stick ($\frac{1}{4}$ cup) salted butter, softened**

Yield: 12 to 16 servings

- Preheat oven to 350°F.
- MAKE THE CRUST: Use a blender or a food processor with a metal blade to grind cookies into fine crumbs. Add butter and blend until smooth. Press crust into bottom of a 9-inch springform pan. Refrigerate while preparing mousse.
- MAKE THE FILLING: In a large bowl with an electric mixer, beat the cream cheese until very smooth. Add sugars and sour cream, and blend thoroughly. Add eggs and beat until mixture is smooth.
- Add melted chocolate, coffee, and vanilla, again blending ingredients until smooth. Pour filling into prepared pan, and bake in middle of oven for 50 to 60 minutes.
- Turn off oven, crack door 1 inch, and leave cheesecake in oven 1 hour to set. Then remove from oven and cool to room temperature.
- MAKE THE GLAZE: In a small saucepan melt chocolate and butter over low heat; stir until smooth. Pour glaze over top of cheesecake and smooth with a metal spatula. Refrigerate 3 to 4 hours or until firm. Cut and serve.

When baked cheesecake has cooled, pour chocolate-butter glaze over the top, and smooth with a metal spatula to form a thin chocolate frosting.

Chocolate Chip Cheesecake

CRUST
5 ounces chocolate cookie crumbs
(about 1 cup)
2 tablespoons salted butter, softened

FILLING
16 ounces cream cheese, softened
1 cup granulated sugar
16 ounces sour cream (about 2 cups)
3 large eggs
1 tablespoon vanilla extract
9 ounces semisweet chocolate chips,
divided (about 1½ cups)

Yield: 12 to 16 servings

- Preheat oven to 350°F.
- PREPARE THE CRUST: Grind cookies into fine crumbs using a blender or a food processor fitted with a metal blade. Add butter and blend until smooth. Press crust into bottom of 9-inch springform pan, and refrigerate while preparing the filling.
- PREPARE THE FILLING: Beat cream cheese until smooth in a large bowl using an electric mixer. Blend in sugar and sour cream. Add the eggs and vanilla, and mix until smooth.

- Using a wooden spoon, stir in 1 cup of the chocolate chips. Pour filling into the crust-lined pan, and smooth top with a spatula. Sprinkle the remaining ½ cup chocolate chips evenly over the top. Bake 30 to 40 minutes. Turn oven off and leave cheesecake in oven for 1 hour to set. Remove from oven and chill in refrigerator until firm, about 3 to 4 hours.

Chocolate Shortbread

CHOCOLATE SHORTBREAD

1½ sticks (¾ cup) unsalted butter, softened
¾ cup confectioners' sugar, sifted
2 teaspoons vanilla extract
1 cup plus 2 tablespoons all-purpose flour
½ cup unsweetened cocoa powder
2 ounces semisweet chocolate, finely grated

WHITE AND DARK GANACHES

6 ounces white chocolate, coarsely chopped
6 ounces semisweet chocolate, coarsely chopped
1 tablespoon granulated sugar
⅔ cup heavy cream
2 tablespoons unsalted butter

Yield: 8 servings

- BAKE THE SHORTBREAD: Preheat the oven to 350°F. Generously grease a 9-inch glass pie plate.
- In a large bowl, beat the butter until creamy. Beat in the confectioners' sugar until well combined. Beat in the vanilla.
- In a small bowl, combine the flour and cocoa. Add the flour-cocoa mixture and the grated chocolate to the dough and beat in just until combined. The mixture will be crumbly.
- Using your hands, shape the dough into a large disk. Place the disk in the prepared pie plate and press it evenly over the bottom of the plate (do not go up the sides). With a fork, prick the dough all the way through, at ½-inch intervals.
- Bake for 25 to 30 minutes, or until just set. Cool in the pie plate on a rack for 10 minutes. While the shortbread is still warm, cut into 8 wedges with a thin, sharp knife. Let the wedges cool completely in the pan.

- MAKE THE GANACHES: Place the white chocolate and semisweet chocolate in two separate medium bowls; add the sugar to the semisweet chocolate. In a small saucepan, bring the cream and butter to a simmer. Pour ⅓ cup of the hot cream over the white chocolate. Pour the remaining ⅓ cup cream over the semisweet chocolate. Let both stand, covered, for 5 minutes; stir until smooth. Let cool to room temperature, then refrigerate until slightly firm, about 20 minutes. Whisk the ganaches to a consistency thick enough to be piped through a pastry bag.
- Place the white and dark ganaches in pastry bags fitted with a #21 star tip. Pipe alternating rows of white and dark ganache rosettes, starting with white ganache at the wider end of the shortbread.

Chocolate Caramel Custard

CARAMEL
1½ cups granulated sugar
¼ cup water

CHOCOLATE CUSTARD
8 egg yolks
½ cup granulated sugar
2 cups light cream

6 ounces semisweet chocolate, finely chopped
1 teaspoon vanilla extract

Whipped cream and chocolate shavings, for garnish

Yield: 8 servings

- Preheat the oven to 325°F.
- MAKE THE CARAMEL: In a small heavy saucepan, dissolve the sugar in the water over low heat. Bring to a boil over medium-high heat, stirring constantly, then let boil without stirring until the syrup turns a deep amber. Quickly remove from the heat and pour an equal quantity of caramel syrup into each of eight 4-ounce ramekins. Place the ramekins in a large baking dish or roasting pan. Set aside.
- PREPARE THE CHOCOLATE CUSTARD: In a medium bowl, combine the egg yolks and sugar until smooth.
- In a medium saucepan, bring the cream to a simmer. Gradually whisk the hot cream into the yolk-sugar mixture. Add the chocolate and vanilla and stir until smooth.
- Strain the custard mixture through a sieve. Dividing evenly, pour the custard into the prepared ramekins. Pour hot water into the baking dish (or roasting pan) to come halfway up the sides of the ramekins. Bake the custards in the middle of the oven for about 30 minutes, or until they are set. Remove from hot water and set on wire racks to cool to room temperature.
- Cover and refrigerate for at least 4 hours or overnight. Serve with a rosette of whipped cream and chocolate shavings.

Chocolate Chip Biscotti

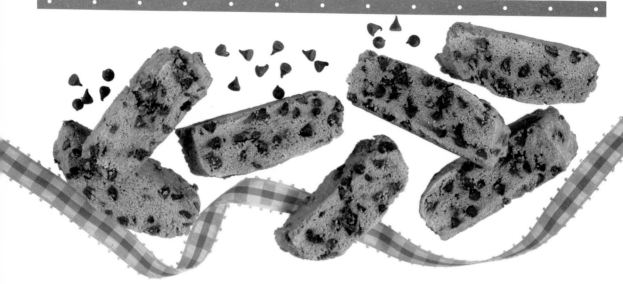

3 cups all-purpose flour
½ cup unsweetened cocoa powder
¾ teaspoon baking powder
⅛ teaspoon salt
3 tablespoons unsalted butter
¾ cup granulated sugar

3 large eggs
1 tablespoon grated orange zest
1 teaspoon vanilla extract
1 cup mini semisweet chocolate chips

Yield: About 3 dozen

- Preheat the oven to 350°F. Spray a baking sheet with nonstick cooking spray.
- In a medium bowl, combine the flour, cocoa, baking powder, and salt and set aside. In another medium bowl with an electric mixer, cream the butter and sugar. Beat in the eggs, one at a time. Beat in the vanilla. Gradually mix in the dry ingredients and orange zest, beating until fully incorporated. Stir in the chocolate chips.
- Divide the dough in half and shape each piece into a log 9 inches long and 3 inches wide. Place the logs on the prepared baking sheet and bake for 30 minutes, or until set. Transfer the logs to a rack and let cool slightly, about 10 minutes. Turn the oven down to 200°F.
- Place the still-warm logs on a cutting board and, with a serrated knife, cut each log on the diagonal into ½-inch slices. Lay the slices on a baking sheet and bake for 5 minutes. Carefully turn the biscotti and bake for another 10 minutes, or until crisp. Transfer to a rack to cool.

After the baked biscotti logs have cooled slightly, cut them with a serrated knife into ½-inch slices. Lay the slices on a baking sheet and bake until crisp.

Caramel-Filled Brownies

BROWNIES
3 ounces unsweetened chocolate
1 stick (½ cup) salted butter, softened
4 large eggs
1½ cups granulated sugar
1 tablespoon vanilla extract
1½ cups all-purpose flour

CARAMEL
½ stick (¼ cup) salted butter
⅓ cup (packed) dark brown sugar
2 tablespoons light corn syrup
1 tablespoon whipping cream

Yield: 16 squares

- Preheat oven to 325°F. Grease an 8-by-8-inch baking pan.
- In a small saucepan, melt chocolate and ½ cup butter over low heat, stirring constantly. Remove from heat.
- Beat eggs in a large bowl using an electric mixer set on high speed until they thicken slightly. Add sugar slowly. Add vanilla and mix well. Add chocolate-butter mixture, and beat on medium until uniformly brown. Add the flour and blend at low speed until just combined. Do not overmix.
- Pour half of the brownie batter into the prepared pan. Smooth top. Bake 15 to 20 minutes or until top is firm.
- PREPARE THE CARAMEL: Heat butter, sugar, and corn syrup in heavy pan over medium heat, stirring constantly until sugar dissolves. Increase heat to high and boil 1½ minutes. Remove from heat and stir in cream. Keep warm.
- Spread warm caramel evenly over top of baked brownie layer. Pour remaining half of brownie mixture over caramel, smoothing the top. Bake an additional 25 to 30 minutes or until toothpick inserted into center comes cleanly out of top brownie layer. (Some caramel may stick to the toothpick.)
- Cool brownies in pan, then cut into squares. Serve at room temperature or chilled.

Fudge-Glazed Chocolate Hazelnut Torte

CAKE

1½ cups hazelnuts, roasted and skinned
4 ounces semisweet chocolate, coarsely chopped
⅓ cup plain, unseasoned dried bread crumbs
1 stick (½ cup) unsalted butter
1¼ cups granulated sugar
6 large eggs, separated
1 teaspoon vanilla extract
½ teaspoon cream of tartar

GANACHE

6 ounces semisweet chocolate, finely chopped
¾ cup heavy cream
1 tablespoon unsalted butter
1 tablespoon granulated sugar

Whipped cream rosettes, for garnish

Yield: 10 to 12 servings

- Preheat the oven to 350°F. Grease and flour the bottom and sides of a 9½-inch springform pan; line the bottom with parchment or wax paper and butter the paper.
- MAKE THE CAKE: In a food processor, process the hazelnuts with the chocolate until finely ground and just beginning to form a paste, about 30 seconds. In a medium bowl, combine the chocolate-hazelnut mixture and bread crumbs.
- In a large bowl, cream the butter with 1 cup of the sugar. Beat in the egg yolks and vanilla. Beat in the chocolate-hazelnut mixture just until blended.
- In a medium bowl, beat the egg whites until foamy. Beat in the cream of tartar, then gradually add the remaining ¼ cup sugar and beat until stiff but not dry peaks form. Stir one-fourth of the egg whites into the batter to lighten it. Gently but thoroughly fold in the remaining egg whites.

- Scrape the batter into the prepared pan. Bake for 45 to 50 minutes, or until a cake tester inserted into the center comes out clean.
- Set on a wire rack to cool for 40 minutes. Loosen the cake with a knife and remove the sides of the pan; let the cake cool completely. Remove the cake from the pan bottom, remove the paper, and set the cake right-side up on a rack. Place the rack over a baking sheet.
- MAKE THE GANACHE: Place the chocolate in a medium bowl. In a small saucepan, bring the cream and butter to a simmer. Stir in the sugar. Pour the hot cream mixture over the chocolate. Let stand, covered, for 5 minutes, then stir until smooth. Let cool to lukewarm.
- Pour the ganache over the cake allowing it to run down the sides. Smooth the top surface. Place in the refrigerator for about 15 minutes to set the ganache. Serve garnished with rosettes of whipped cream.

120

Mrs. Fields' Macadamia Nut Tart

PASTRY CRUST
1¾ cups all-purpose flour
¼ cup granulated sugar
1 stick (½ cup) salted butter, chilled
2 large egg yolks
3 tablespoons ice water

FILLING
1 cup corn syrup
1 stick (½ cup) plus 3 tablespoons salted butter

1 cup granulated sugar
2 tablespoons unsulfurized molasses
¼ teaspoon salt
2 large eggs, lightly beaten
1 teaspoon vanilla extract
2½ cups unsalted dry-roasted macadamia nuts
Whipped cream (optional)

Yield: 12 servings

- PREPARE THE CRUST: Combine flour, sugar, and butter, and work with a pastry cutter until dough resembles coarse meal. Add egg yolks and water, and mix with a fork just until dough can be shaped into a ball. Or, using a food processor fitted with a metal blade, combine flour, sugar, and butter. Process until dough resembles coarse meal. Add egg yolks and water and process just until a ball begins to form.
- Shape dough into a disk and wrap tightly in plastic wrap or plastic bag. Chill in refrigerator 1 hour or until firm.
- PREPARE THE FILLING: Combine the corn syrup, butter, sugar, molasses, and salt in a double boiler. Bring to a boil over medium heat, stirring occasionally. Remove from heat and cool to room temperature. Once cool, add the eggs and vanilla and stir until smooth. Set syrup mixture aside until ready to use. (Mixture can be made up to 2 days in advance and refrigerated until ready to use.)
- ASSEMBLE THE TART: Preheat oven to 300°F. Spray nonstick cooking spray on an 8- or 9-inch tart pan with a removable bottom.
- On a floured board using a floured rolling pin, roll out dough to a 10-inch circle, ¼ inch thick. Place pastry in pan, lightly pressing it into the bottom and sides. Roll off excess dough from the top edge with rolling pin.
- Fill the pastry shell with the macadamia nuts. Pour filling over nuts and bake 90 minutes or until golden brown. Let pie cool, remove sides of pan and garnish with whipped cream, if desired.

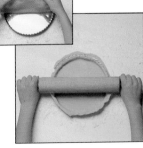

Fold the dough in half, then drape it over the prepared tart pan (right, top). Gently press the dough into the pan. Be sure that there is enough dough pressed into the fluted edges to support the filling when baked. Use a rolling pin to roll off the excess dough (right).

White Chocolate Soufflé

SOUFFLÉ
8 ounces white chocolate, coarsely chopped
½ cup granulated sugar
⅓ cup milk
4 large egg yolks
1 teaspoon vanilla extract
6 large egg whites
½ teaspoon cream of tartar

RASPBERRY SAUCE
One 12-ounce package unsweetened frozen
raspberries
¼ cup granulated sugar
1 tablespoon orange juice
Confectioners' sugar, for dusting

Yield: 6 to 8 servings

- MAKE THE SOUFFLÉ: In a double boiler, melt the white chocolate over hot, not simmering, water. Set aside to cool slightly.
- Preheat the oven to 350°F. Butter and sugar a ½-quart soufflé dish.
- In a small saucepan, combine the sugar and milk. Cook over medium heat, stirring constantly, until the sugar dissolves, about 3 minutes. Transfer the mixture to a medium bowl. Whisk in the melted white chocolate, egg yolks, and vanilla until well blended.
- In a medium bowl, beat the egg whites and cream of tartar until stiff peaks form. Fold the egg whites into the white chocolate mixture.
- Spoon the mixture into the prepared soufflé dish. With a knife, cut a circle into the top of the soufflé 1 inch in from the edge and about 1 inch deep. Bake the soufflé for 25 to 30 minutes, or until the top is puffed, golden brown, and firm (the inside will still be jiggly).
- MEANWHILE, MAKE THE SAUCE: Drain the berries in a fine-mesh sieve set over a bowl; press gently on the berries to remove as much juice as possible. Transfer the juice to a small saucepan and simmer until reduced to about ⅓ cup. Return the reduced juice to the bowl and stir in the sugar and orange juice. With a wooden spoon press the raspberries through the strainer into the bowl. Stir to combine the purée with the juice.
- Remove the soufflé from the oven, dust with confectioners' sugar, and serve immediately with the raspberry sauce.

Debbi's Deadly Chocolate Muffins

12 ounces semisweet chocolate, coarsely
chopped
1 stick ($\frac{1}{2}$ cup) unsalted butter
$\frac{1}{2}$ cup sour cream
1 cup sifted cake flour
$\frac{1}{2}$ teaspoon baking soda
$\frac{1}{4}$ teaspoon salt
4 large eggs

$\frac{1}{2}$ cup (packed) light brown sugar
1 teaspoon vanilla extract
$1\frac{1}{4}$ cups semisweet chocolate chips
$\frac{1}{4}$ cup coarsely chopped macadamia nuts
$\frac{1}{4}$ cup white chocolate chips

Yield: 12 muffins

- Preheat the oven to 350°F. Lightly oil the top surface of a 12-cup muffin tin. Line the cups with paper liners.
- In a double boiler, melt the chopped semisweet chocolate with the butter and stir until smooth. Remove from the heat and stir in the sour cream.
- In a small bowl, whisk together the flour, baking soda, and salt.
- In a large bowl with an electric mixer, beat the eggs and sugar until light and pale, about 5 minutes. Beat in the chocolate mixture and the vanilla. Add the flour mixture and 1 cup of the semisweet chocolate chips.
- Spoon the batter evenly into the prepared muffin cups. Top with the remaining $\frac{1}{4}$ cup semisweet chips, the macadamia nuts, and the white chocolate chips. Bake for 20 to 25 minutes, or until the centers are set.
- Set the muffin tin on a wire rack to cool for 15 minutes. Then remove the muffins to cool completely.

Chocolate Pudding Soufflé Cake

CAKE
4 tablespoons (¼ cup) unsalted butter
3 ounces unsweetened chocolate
½ cup cake flour
½ teaspoon baking powder
¼ teaspoon salt
6 large eggs—3 separated, 3 whole
1 cup granulated sugar
¼ teaspoon cream of tartar

PUDDING
5 large egg yolks
½ cup granulated sugar
2 tablespoons cornstarch
2½ cups heavy cream
8 ounces semisweet chocolate, finely
chopped
2 teaspoons vanilla extract

Yield: One 9-inch layer cake

- Preheat the oven to 375°F. Grease a 9-inch springform pan.
- MAKE THE CAKE: In a double boiler, melt the butter and unsweetened chocolate. Stir until smooth, then set aside. In a small bowl, combine the flour, baking powder, and salt. In a large bowl with an electric mixer, beat the 3 whole eggs and 3 egg yolks with ¾ cup of the sugar until pale and lemon-colored. Slowly beat in the chocolate mixture. Then beat in the flour mixture.
- In a medium bowl, beat the egg whites until foamy. Add the cream of tartar and beat until soft peaks form. Beat in the remaining ¼ cup sugar until stiff glossy peaks form. Stir one-third of the egg whites into the batter to lighten it. Gently and thoroughly fold in the remaining whites. Transfer the batter to the prepared pan and smooth the top.

- Bake for 40 to 50 minutes, or until the center is set. Transfer to a wire rack to cool to room temperature. Refrigerate until firm.
- MEANWHILE, MAKE THE PUDDING: In a medium bowl, lightly beat the egg yolks. In a heavy medium saucepan, whisk together the sugar and cornstarch. Gradually whisk in the cream. Bring the mixture to a boil over low heat, whisking constantly.
- Very gradually whisk the hot cream into the egg yolks, then return the mixture to the saucepan and cook over very low heat, whisking constantly, until the pudding is very thick and steamy; do not let it boil. Remove the pudding from the heat, stir in the chocolate and vanilla, and stir until melted and smooth. Transfer the pudding to a bowl, place a piece of plastic wrap directly on the surface, and refrigerate until cold, at least 2 hours.

The Ultimate Ice Cream Pie

COOKIE CRUMB CRUST
1¼ cups chocolate-chip cookie crumbs

FUDGE SAUCE
2 ounces semisweet chocolate, chopped
2½ tablespoons unsalted butter
¼ cup plus 2 tablespoons granulated sugar
2 tablespoons unsweetened cocoa powder
2 tablespoons corn syrup
¼ cup plus 2 tablespoons water
1 teaspoon vanilla extract

CARAMEL SAUCE
½ cup granulated sugar
2 tablespoons water
¼ cup cream, scalded
2 tablespoons unsalted butter, softened

FILLING
1 cup mini marshmallows
1 cup semisweet chocolate chips
3 cups vanilla ice cream, softened in the refrigerator

Yield: One 9-inch pie

- Preheat the oven to 325°F.
- MAKE THE CRUST: Press the cookie crumbs into the bottom and up the sides of a 9-inch pie plate. Bake for 10 minutes. Cool the crust to room temperature.
- PREPARE THE FUDGE SAUCE: In a small saucepan, melt the chocolate and butter over low heat; stir until smooth. Add the sugar, cocoa, corn syrup, and water and cook until the sugar dissolves. Bring the mixture to a boil and cook at a low boil, without stirring, until the sauce is thick and smooth, about 15 minutes. Remove from the heat and stir in the vanilla. Set aside to cool to lukewarm.
- MAKE THE CARAMEL SAUCE: In a heavy medium saucepan, dissolve the sugar in the water over low heat, stirring constantly. Bring to a boil over medium-high heat, then let boil, without stirring, until the syrup turns a light amber.

While the syrup is boiling, brush down the sides of the pan from time to time with a wet pastry brush to prevent crystals from forming. Remove the pan from the heat and stir in the hot cream (it will bubble rapidly). Stir in the butter and continue stirring the sauce until smooth. Cool the sauce to lukewarm.
- ASSEMBLE: Pour the fudge sauce into the pie crust. Chill in the freezer until the sauce is set, about 15 minutes. In a medium bowl, stir the marshmallows and chocolate chips into the softened ice cream. Spread the ice cream mixture over the fudge layer and smooth the top. Place in the freezer until set, about 30 minutes.
- Dip a fork into the caramel sauce and drizzle it in a crisscross pattern over the top of the pie. Return to the freezer for 1 hour to set. Cut the pie into wedges with a sharp knife and serve immediately.

Raspberry and White Chocolate Tart

CHOCOLATE TART SHELL
1 cup all-purpose flour
¼ cup unsweetened cocoa powder
4 tablespoons granulated sugar
¼ teaspoon salt
6 tablespoons cold unsalted butter, cut into small pieces
1 large egg yolk
1 teaspoon vanilla extract
2 to 3 tablespoons ice water

WHITE CHOCOLATE CUSTARD
1 cup heavy cream
2 egg yolks
1 tablespoon granulated sugar
1 tablespoon cornstarch
6 ounces white chocolate, finely chopped

1 pint fresh raspberries
Confectioners' sugar, for dusting

Yield: One 9-inch tart

- MAKE THE TART SHELL: In a food processor, combine the flour, cocoa, sugar, and salt and process briefly. Add the butter and pulse until the mixture resembles coarse meal. In a small bowl, lightly beat the egg yolk with the vanilla. With the machine running, drizzle in the egg yolk mixture through the feed tube, then drizzle enough of the water so that the dough begins to gather into a ball. Scrape the dough from the work bowl, flatten into a disk, and wrap with plastic wrap. Chill for 1 hour.

- PREPARE THE WHITE CHOCOLATE CUSTARD: In a small heavy saucepan, stir together the sugar and cornstarch. Gradually whisk in the cream. Bring to a boil over medium-low heat, stirring constantly. In a small bowl, beat the egg yolks. Gradually whisk the cream into the yolks and return the mixture to the saucepan. Cook over low heat, stirring constantly, until the custard is very thick and steamy; do not allow it to boil. Remove from the heat and stir in the white chocolate. Transfer to a bowl, place a sheet of plastic wrap directly on the surface of the custard, and refrigerate until well chilled, about 2 hours.

- Remove the dough from the refrigerator and let stand for 10 minutes. On a lightly floured surface, roll the dough out to an 11-inch round. Transfer to a 9-inch tart pan with a removable bottom and press dough into the bottom and sides. Freeze the tart shell for 15 minutes.

- Meanwhile, preheat the oven to 400°F. Bake the tart shell for 18 minutes, or until set. Cool on a wire rack.

- ASSEMBLE THE TART: Spread the white chocolate custard evenly into the tart shell. Arrange the raspberries over the surface of the tart and dust with confectioners' sugar.

Chocolate Pecan Tartlets

<u>PASTRY</u>
2 cups all-purpose flour
2 sticks (1 cup) salted butter
2 large egg yolks
2 to 3 tablespoons ice water

<u>FILLING</u>
1 stick (¹/₂ cup) salted butter
4 ounces unsweetened baking chocolate
2 large eggs
1 cup (packed) dark brown sugar

¹/₂ cup corn syrup
2 teaspoons vanilla extract
1¹/₂ cups pecans, chopped

<u>TOPPING</u>
24 pecan halves
¹/₂ cup heavy cream
¹/₄ cup granulated sugar
1 teaspoon vanilla extract

Yield: Twenty-four 2¹/₂-inch tartlets

- PREPARE PASTRY: In medium bowl, combine flour and butter with pastry cutter until dough resembles coarse meal. Add egg yolks and water, then mix with a fork just until dough can be shaped into a ball.
- Gather dough into a ball. Wrap tightly in plastic wrap or a plastic bag. Refrigerate until firm—about 1 hour.
- PREPARE FILLING: In a 2-quart saucepan combine butter and chocolate, stirring constantly over low heat. Transfer to medium bowl and let cool for 5 minutes. With an electric mixer on medium speed, beat eggs into chocolate mixture. Add sugar, corn syrup, and vanilla, and blend on low speed until smooth. Fold in pecans.
- Preheat oven to 350°F.
- ASSEMBLE TARTLETS: On lightly floured counter or board, use a lightly floured rolling

pin to roll out dough to ¹/₈-inch thickness. Using a 2¹/₂-inch fluted tartlet pan as a guide, cut dough ¹/₄ inch around entire edge. Repeat with remaining dough. Lay dough rounds in tartlet pans and press in firmly.
- Fill pans ²/₃ full of chocolate pecan filling. Place on baking sheet to catch any drips. Bake for 30 to 35 minutes, or until filling is set and does not look wet.
- While still warm, place a pecan half in center of each tartlet. Meanwhile, chill mixing bowl and beaters in freezer.
- PREPARE TOPPING: In a medium bowl with electric mixer set on high, beat cream, sugar, and vanilla until stiff peaks form. Do not overbeat. Transfer the whipped topping to a pastry bag fitted with a medium star tip, and pipe decorative topping onto each tartlet.

Chocolate Custard-Filled Meringues

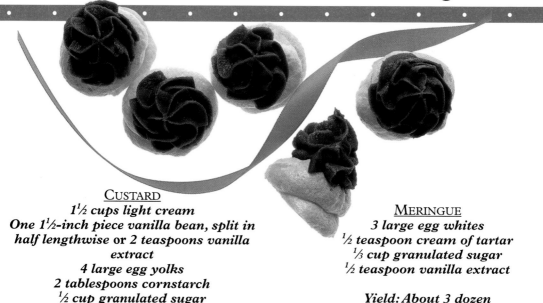

CUSTARD
1½ cups light cream
One 1½-inch piece vanilla bean, split in
half lengthwise **or** *2 teaspoons vanilla*
extract
4 large egg yolks
2 tablespoons cornstarch
½ cup granulated sugar
6 ounces semisweet chocolate chips
(about 1 cup)

MERINGUE
3 large egg whites
½ teaspoon cream of tartar
⅓ cup granulated sugar
½ teaspoon vanilla extract

Yield: About 3 dozen

- MAKE THE CHOCOLATE CUSTARD: In a medium saucepan, scald cream with vanilla bean.
- In a small bowl, lightly beat egg yolks with cornstarch until no lumps remain. Add sugar, then slowly whisk in 1 cup of the hot cream. Pour yolk-cream mixture back into the saucepan and cook over medium-low heat, stirring constantly until mixture thickens enough to coat the back of a spoon. Do not boil or the egg will curdle.
- Transfer custard into a medium bowl, and stir in chocolate chips until melted. If you are using vanilla extract, stir it in with the chocolate chips.
- MAKE THE MERINGUE: In a medium bowl with an electric mixer on high speed, beat egg whites until foamy. Add cream of tartar and half of the sugar; continue mixing until thickened—about

5 minutes. While still beating, add the remaining sugar slowly until stiff peaks form. Finally, beat in the vanilla. Do not overbeat or peaks may fall.
- Transfer meringue to pastry bag with a large plain tip. Pipe 1-inch balls onto lightly greased and foil-lined baking sheets. (Too much butter on the sheets will cause meringues to slide.) If you don't have a pastry bag, drop meringue by rounded teaspoons.
- With your index finger coated in flour, poke holes in center of each meringue, about ½ inch in diameter. This will hold the custard after the meringues are baked.
- Preheat oven to 225°F. Set meringues out to dry for 45 minutes. Then bake for 35 to 45 minutes, just until meringue turns golden brown.
- Cool meringues to room temperature. With pastry bag or small spoon, fill meringues with chocolate custard.

Slowly add sugar to the thickened egg whites (far left), and beat until stiff peaks form. Continuous beating gives the meringue the air it needs to stand up (left), but overbeating may cause it to fall.

Caramel Chocolate Tartlets

PASTRY
1½ cups all-purpose flour
¼ cup granulated sugar
1 stick (½ cup) salted butter, chilled
2 large egg yolks
1 teaspoon vanilla extract
4 to 5 tablespoons ice water

CARAMEL FILLING
1½ sticks (¾ cup) salted butter
1 cup (packed) dark brown sugar
⅓ cup light corn syrup
3 tablespoons heavy cream
One 16-ounce solid semisweet or milk chocolate bar, room temperature

Yield: 8 tartlets

- In medium bowl, combine flour, sugar, and butter with a pastry cutter until dough resembles coarse meal. Add egg yolks and vanilla. Gradually add ice water until dough can be shaped into a ball. Or, use a food processor fitted with a metal blade to combine flour, sugar, and butter until dough resembles coarse meal. Add egg yolks, vanilla, and ice water by tablespoons, and process until dough begins to form a ball.
- Flatten dough into a disk and wrap tightly in plastic wrap or place in plastic bag. Chill 1 hour or until firm.
- On floured board using a floured rolling pin, roll out dough to ¼ inch thickness. Cut 4-inch rounds to fit into 3½-inch-diameter tart pans. Gently press into tart pans and place in refrig-

erator for 15 minutes. Preheat oven to 400°F.
- Remove tart shells from refrigerator and prick bottom with a fork. Bake 13 to 15 minutes or until edges begin to turn golden brown. Cool tart shells to room temperature.
- PREPARE THE CARAMEL FILLING: Combine butter, brown sugar, and corn syrup in a heavy 2-quart saucepan. Place over medium heat, and stir constantly until sugar dissolves. Turn heat to high and boil without stirring for 2 minutes, or until large bubbles form.
- Remove from heat and stir in cream. Cool caramel 5 minutes and then pour into tart shells. Cool caramel tartlets to room temperature. Use a vegetable peeler to slowly and carefully shave curls from the chocolate bar. Sprinkle tartlets with chocolate curls.

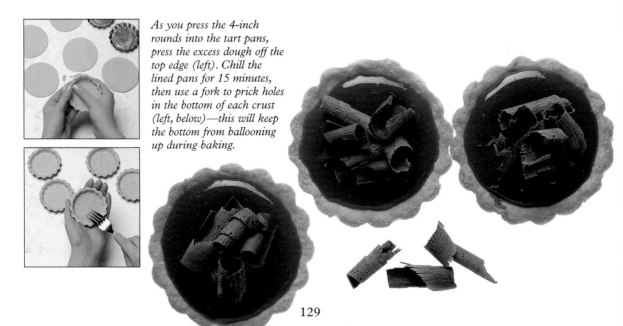

As you press the 4-inch rounds into the tart pans, press the excess dough off the top edge (left). Chill the lined pans for 15 minutes, then use a fork to prick holes in the bottom of each crust (left, below)—this will keep the bottom from ballooning up during baking.

Lemon Custard Cake

CAKE
1½ cups cake flour
1 cup granulated sugar
I teaspoon baking powder
½ teaspoon salt
1½ sticks (¾ cup) unsalted butter, softened
¼ cup sour cream
2 large eggs, at room temperature
¼ cup lemon juice
2 teaspoons grated lemon zest
½ teaspoon lemon extract

VANILLA CUSTARD
1 cup heavy cream
1 large egg

2 large egg yolks
⅓ cup granulated sugar
1 tablespoon plus 2 teaspoons cornstarch
1 teaspoon vanilla extract

CHOCOLATE GANACHE
6 ounces semisweet chocolate, finely chopped
¾ cup heavy cream
2 tablespoons unsalted butter
2 tablespoons granulated sugar

Yield: One 9-inch layer cake

- Preheat the oven to 350°F. Grease a 9-inch cake pan, line the bottom with a circle of wax paper, then grease and flour the paper.
- MAKE THE CAKE: In a large bowl, mix the flour, sugar, baking powder, and salt. Add the butter, sour cream, and 1 egg. Mix until just blended. Add the remaining egg, the lemon juice, zest, and extract. Beat until smooth.
- Scrape batter into pan and bake for 40 to 45 minutes, or until top is golden and a cake tester inserted in the center comes out clean. Set the cake pan on a wire rack to cool for 20 minutes. Then invert cake onto rack to cool completely. Wrap cake in plastic wrap and chill in freezer until slightly firm, about 15 minutes.
- MEANWHILE, MAKE THE CUSTARD: In a small saucepan, bring cream to a simmer. In a bowl, beat whole egg, egg yolks, sugar, and cornstarch together until light and lemon-colored, about 3 minutes. Gradually whisk hot cream into egg mixture to warm it. Transfer

warmed egg mixture to saucepan and cook over medium heat, stirring constantly, until thick, about 2 minutes. Remove from heat and stir in vanilla. Strain the custard through a fine sieve and set in a large bowl of ice water to quick-cool to room temperature. Cover and refrigerate until thoroughly chilled.
- PREPARE THE GANACHE: Place the chocolate in a medium bowl. In a small saucepan, bring the cream and butter to a simmer. Stir in the sugar. Pour the hot cream mixture over the chocolate. Let stand, covered, for 5 minutes, then stir until smooth. Let cool to room temperature.
- ASSEMBLE: With a long serrated knife, slice chilled cake horizontally into two layers. Place bottom cake layer on a 9-inch cardboard round. Place layer on a rack set over a cookie sheet. Spread top of cake with the chilled vanilla custard. Gently top with the second cake layer. Spread the ganache evenly over sides and top of cake. Refrigerate for 20 minutes to set.

Chocolate Raspberry Rhapsody

CHOCOLATE RING
1¼ cups semisweet chocolate chips
1 cup granulated sugar
½ cup boiling water
2 sticks (1 cup) unsalted butter, softened
4 large eggs
2 tablespoons raspberry liqueur
2 teaspoons vanilla extract
⅛ teaspoon salt

RASPBERRY CREAM
1 cup heavy cream
2 tablespoons seedless red raspberry jam
2 tablespoons granulated sugar
2 teaspoons vanilla extract
Fresh raspberries, for garnish

Yield: 16 servings

- Preheat the oven to 350°F. Spray a 5-cup ring mold with nonstick cooking spray.
- MAKE THE CHOCOLATE RING: In a food processor, combine the chocolate chips and sugar, then process until finely chopped. Add the boiling water and process until melted and smooth. Add the butter in three additions, processing briefly each time. Add the eggs, liqueur, vanilla, and salt. Process until well blended.
- Pour the mixture into the prepared ring mold. Place the mold in a larger pan and fill the pan with 2 inches of boiling water. Bake for 1 hour, or until firm to the touch; a knife inserted into the center should come out clean.
- Remove the mold from the water bath and let cool for 1 hour on a rack. Cover and refrigerate for at least 3 hours.
- MAKE THE RASPBERRY CREAM: In a small bowl, beat the cream with the jam, sugar, and vanilla until soft peaks form.
- ASSEMBLE: Run a knife around the edges of the mold and invert the ring onto a serving dish. Pipe a ring of raspberry cream rosettes around the base of the ring. Fill the center of the ring with the remaining raspberry cream. Garnish the ring with fresh raspberries.

Double-Fudge Chip Cake

CAKE

3 ounces unsweetened chocolate, finely
chopped
2¼ cups sifted cake flour
2 teaspoons baking soda
½ teaspoon salt
1 stick (½ cup) salted butter, softened
2¼ cups (packed) light brown sugar
3 large eggs, at room temperature
1½ teaspoons vanilla extract
1 cup sour cream
1 cup boiling water

FROSTING

8 ounces unsweetened chocolate, finely
chopped
2 sticks (1 cup) unsalted butter, softened
2 pounds confectioners' sugar
1 cup heavy cream
4 teaspoons vanilla extract
6 ounces milk chocolate chips (1 cup)
1 package chocolate kisses, for garnish

Yield: One 9-inch layer cake

- Preheat the oven to 350°F. Grease and flour three 9-inch cake pans.
- MAKE THE CAKE: In a double boiler, melt the chocolate over hot, not simmering, water. Set aside to cool.
- In a medium bowl, combine the flour, baking soda, and salt.
- In a large bowl with an electric mixer, cream the butter. Add the brown sugar and then the eggs, one at a time, blending well after each addition. Beat at high speed for 5 minutes. Beat in the vanilla and the melted chocolate.
- Beat in portions of the flour mixture alternately with the sour cream, beginning and ending with the flour mixture; beat well after each addition.
- Stir in the boiling water and pour the batter at once into the prepared pans. Bake for 35 minutes, or until the center springs back when touched lightly. Set the cake pans on a rack to

cool for 10 minutes. Then invert the cakes onto the racks to cool completely.
- PREPARE THE FROSTING: In a double boiler, melt the chocolate with the butter. Set aside to cool to room temperature.
- In a medium bowl with an electric mixer, blend the confectioners' sugar, cream, and vanilla until smooth. Add the cooled chocolate mixture and mix at low speed until blended. Place the frosting in the refrigerator until thick and firm yet still easy to spread, 20 to 30 minutes.
- ASSEMBLE: Place one cake layer upside down on a cake dish. Spread one-fourth of frosting on top and sprinkle with ½ cup of the chips. Add a second cake layer upside down and frost with another one-fourth of the frosting and the remaining ½ cup chips. Add the top layer upside down and frost the top and sides of the cake with the remaining frosting. Garnish the cake with the chocolate kisses.

Chocolate Cream Roll

CAKE

**6 ounces semisweet chocolate, coarsely
chopped
6 large eggs, separated
$\frac{1}{4}$ cup granulated sugar
1 teaspoon vanilla extract
$\frac{1}{2}$ teaspoon cream of tartar**

CREAM FILLING

**1 cup heavy cream
2 tablespoons confectioners' sugar
1 teaspoon vanilla extract
2 teaspoons unsweetened cocoa powder
Fudge Sauce (page 136)**

Yield: 12 servings

- Preheat the oven to 350°F. Line a 12-by-17-inch jelly-roll pan with foil. Grease and flour the foil.
- MAKE THE CAKE: In a double boiler, melt the chocolate over hot, not simmering, water. Set aside to cool slightly.
- In a medium bowl with an electric mixer, beat the egg yolks and granulated sugar until light and lemon-colored, about 5 minutes. Blend in the chocolate and vanilla. Set aside.
- In another medium bowl, beat the egg whites until soft peaks form. Add the cream of tartar and beat until stiff peaks form. Stir one-fourth of the beaten whites into the chocolate mixture to lighten it. Gently but thoroughly fold in the remaining whites. Immediately transfer the batter to the prepared pan and smooth the top of the batter.

- Bake for 15 minutes, or until the center of the cake springs back when lightly pressed. Cover the cake with a damp kitchen towel and cool to room temperature on a rack.
- PREPARE THE FILLING: In a medium bowl, whip the cream with the confectioners' sugar and vanilla until stiff peaks form.
- ASSEMBLE: Very gently lift the cake out of the pan along with the foil. Dust the top of the cake evenly with the cocoa. Spread the surface with the whipped cream, leaving a 1-inch border along the cake edges. With a long end toward you, roll up the cake, gently removing the foil as you go.
- To serve, drizzle some of the Fudge Sauce onto a plate and place a slice of the cake roll on top of the sauce. Serve any remaining sauce at the table.

Sweetie Pie Cookie Dough Ice Cream

2 ounces unsweetened chocolate
1¾ cups semisweet chocolate chips
1 stick (½ cup) unsalted butter
1 cup granulated sugar
2 teaspoons vanilla extract
2 tablespoons water
1 cup all-purpose flour
½ cup white chocolate chips

¼ cup milk chocolate chips
2 quarts chocolate or vanilla ice cream,
slightly softened
Fudge Sauce (page 136) and mixed
chocolate chips, for garnish

Yield: About 3 quarts

- In a double boiler, melt the unsweetened chocolate and ¾ cup of the chocolate chips over hot, not simmering, water. Stir until smooth.
- In a medium bowl, cream the butter and sugar. Add the vanilla and water and beat until smooth. Beat in the melted chocolate. Add the flour, white chocolate chips, milk chocolate chips, and remaining 1 cup semisweet choco-late chips; mix at low speed until the chips are evenly distributed throughout the dough.
- Drop the dough by the teaspoon into the softened ice cream and stir to mix, partially blending the dough into the ice cream. Return to the freezer to firm up before serving.
- Serve the ice cream with Fudge Sauce and a sprinkling of chocolate chips.

Frozen Chocolate Mint Mousse

8 ounces semisweet chocolate, finely
chopped
2 large egg whites
2 pinches of cream of tartar
½ cup granulated sugar
¼ cup water
1 cup heavy cream, chilled

3 tablespoons crème de menthe
½ cup semisweet chocolate chips, coarsely
chopped
Whipped cream and fresh mint,
for garnish

Yield: 4 to 6 servings

- In a double boiler, melt the chocolate over hot, not simmering, water. Set aside to cool slightly.
- Meanwhile, beat the egg whites with a pinch of cream of tartar until stiff peaks form.
- In a small saucepan, boil the sugar and water with another pinch of cream of tartar until it reaches 234°F to 240°F on a candy thermometer (soft-ball stage), 10 to 12 minutes.
- With the mixer going, carefully pour the hot sugar syrup into the egg whites to make a stiff, glossy meringue. Fold the melted chocolate into the meringue to make chewy lumps.

- In a medium bowl, beat the heavy cream until soft peaks form. Add the crème de menthe and keep beating until stiff peaks form. Fold the chopped chocolate chips into the whipped cream, then fold the whipped cream into the chocolate meringue, leaving streaks of whipped cream. Spoon the mousse into individual dessert bowls or glasses, cover with plastic wrap and freeze until firm, about 2 hours.
- Serve garnished with whipped cream and fresh mint.

Creamy Mocha Ice Cream Shake

FUDGE SAUCE
*4 ounces semisweet chocolate, coarsely
chopped
5 tablespoons unsalted butter
$\frac{1}{4}$ cup unsweetened cocoa powder
$\frac{3}{4}$ cup granulated sugar
$\frac{3}{4}$ cup water
$\frac{1}{4}$ cup light corn syrup
2 teaspoons vanilla extract*

SHAKES
*$\frac{1}{2}$ cup milk
1 teaspoon instant coffee granules
1 teaspoon coffee liqueur
(optional)
1$\frac{1}{2}$ cups vanilla ice cream
Whipped cream and chocolate shavings,
for garnish*

Yield: 2 servings

- MAKE THE FUDGE SAUCE: In a heavy medium saucepan, combine the chocolate, butter, cocoa, sugar, water, and corn syrup. Whisk over medium-high heat until the chocolate and butter are melted and the sugar is dissolved. When the sauce just comes to a boil, reduce the heat to low and cook at a low boil for 8 to 10 minutes; the sauce will thicken as it cools. Add the vanilla and stir to combine. Let cool to room temperature, then store in the refrigerator until ready to use. (This fudge sauce recipe makes enough for six ice cream shakes. If you are only making two, refrigerate remaining fudge sauce and keep on hand as an ice cream topping.)
- MAKE THE SHAKES: In a blender, combine $\frac{1}{2}$ cup of the fudge sauce, the milk, coffee granules, and coffee liqueur (if using). Process until smooth. Add the ice cream and blend until smooth and thick.
- Pour the shakes into tall glasses and garnish with whipped cream rosettes and chocolate shavings.

Homestyle Chocolate Pudding

1 cup granulated sugar
¼ cup cornstarch
¼ cup plus 2 tablespoons unsweetened cocoa powder
⅛ teaspoon salt

4 cups heavy cream
2 large egg yolks, lightly beaten
2 teaspoons vanilla extract

Yield: 4 to 6 servings

- In a heavy medium saucepan, stir together the sugar, cornstarch, cocoa powder, and salt. Gradually whisk in the cream and egg yolks.
- Place over medium heat and cook, stirring frequently, until the mixture comes to a boil, about 20 minutes. Simmer, stirring constantly, for 1 minute, then remove from the heat and stir in the vanilla.
- Transfer the pudding to a serving bowl, cover, and refrigerate until well chilled.
- NOTE: For a light version of the pudding, use low-fat (1%) milk in place of the heavy cream and increase the cornstarch to ¼ cup plus 1 tablespoon.

Super Mud Pie

CRUST
2 cups chocolate wafer crumbs
4 tablespoons ($\frac{1}{4}$ cup) unsalted butter, melted

CARAMEL SAUCE
$\frac{1}{2}$ cup granulated sugar
3 tablespoons water
$\frac{1}{2}$ cup heavy cream, scalded
4 tablespoons unsalted butter, softened

ESPRESSO FUDGE SAUCE
4 ounces semisweet chocolate, coarsely chopped

$\frac{1}{4}$ cup unsweetened cocoa powder
4 tablespoons unsalted butter
$\frac{3}{4}$ cup freshly brewed espresso
$\frac{3}{4}$ cup granulated sugar
$\frac{1}{4}$ cup light corn syrup
1 tablespoon coffee liqueur

ASSEMBLY
1 quart vanilla ice cream, softened
$\frac{1}{2}$ cup coarsely chopped toasted macadamia nuts

Yield: 8 to 10 servings

- MAKE THE CRUST: Combine the wafer crumbs and melted butter. Press the mixture into the bottom and partially up the sides of a 9-inch springform pan.
- MAKE THE CARAMEL SAUCE: In a small heavy saucepan, dissolve the sugar in the water over low heat, stirring constantly. Bring to a boil over medium-high heat, then let boil without stirring until the syrup turns a light amber. While the syrup is boiling, brush down the sides of the pan from time to time to prevent crystals from forming. Remove the pan from the heat and stir in the hot cream (be careful, it will bubble rapidly). Continue stirring, over low heat if necessary, until all of the caramel is dissolved into the cream. Stir in the butter and set aside to cool slightly. Pour the warm caramel sauce over the crust and freeze until firm, about 30 minutes.
- MAKE THE ESPRESSO FUDGE SAUCE: In a medium saucepan, combine the chopped chocolate,

cocoa, butter, and espresso. Stir over low heat until smooth. Add the sugar and corn syrup, increase the heat to medium, and stir until the sugar dissolves. Increase the heat until the sauce reaches a low boil. Cook without stirring until the sauce thickens, 12 to 15 minutes. Remove from the heat and stir in the coffee liqueur.
- Cool the sauce to room temperature, then pour 1 cup of the sauce over the caramel layer and return the crust to the freezer. Set the remaining sauce aside and keep just warm enough so it remains pourable.
- ASSEMBLE THE PIE: Spread the softened ice cream over the caramel layer and return to the freezer to firm, about 1 hour. Pour the remaining fudge sauce over the ice cream layer, top with the macadamia nuts, and freeze until firm, about 2 hours.
- SERVE: Wrap a hot, wet towel around the springform for 2 minutes to loosen, then remove the sides of the pan.

Mocha Parfait

*4 ounces semisweet chocolate, coarsely
chopped
8 large egg yolks
⅓ cup light corn syrup
⅓ cup granulated sugar*

*1 tablespoon instant coffee granules
dissolved in 1 tablespoon
coffee liqueur
2 cups heavy cream
Chocolate stick candy, for garnish*

Yield: 8 servings

- In a double boiler, melt the chocolate over hot, not simmering, water. Set aside to cool to room temperature.
- In a medium bowl set over a saucepan of simmering water, combine the egg yolks, corn syrup, and sugar. With an electric mixer, beat the egg-yolk mixture constantly until it is very thick and pale and warm to the touch. Remove the bowl from the water bath and continue beating until the eggs are cool.
- Transfer one-third of the egg mixture to a small bowl and stir in the dissolved coffee.
- Mix the melted chocolate into the egg mixture remaining in the medium bowl.
- In another medium bowl, beat the cream until soft peaks form. With a whisk, beat about ½ cup of the whipped cream into the chocolate mixture to lighten it. Then gently but thoroughly fold in two-thirds of the remaining whipped cream. With a whisk, beat in ⅓ cup whipped cream into the coffee mixture to light-

en it, then gently but thoroughly fold in the remaining whipped cream.
- Spoon half of the chocolate parfait mixture into eight 1-cup parfait glasses. Place in the freezer for 10 minutes to firm (keep the remaining parfait mixtures in the refrigerator).
- Layer all of the coffee mixture into the parfait glasses and return the parfaits to the freezer to firm. Top the parfaits with the remaining chocolate mixture and freeze until completely firm, about 2 hours.
- Serve the parfait with chocolate stick candy.

INDEX

TIME LIFE BOOKS

Time-Life Books is a division of

TIME LIFE INC.

Time-Life Custom Publishing

Vice President and Publisher: Terry Newell

Project Manager: Christopher M. Register

Director of Sales: Neil Levin

Director of New Product Development: Regina Hall

Managing Editor: Donia Ann Steele

Production Manager: Carolyn Bounds

Quality Assurance Manager: James D. King

Mrs. Fields Best Cookie Book Ever!

Editors: Blaine Marshall, Kate Slate

Art Directors: Susan White, Robert Herndon

Photography: Renée Comet, Lisa Koenig

First printing. Printed in U.S.A.

Time-Life is a trademark of Time Warner Inc. U.S.A.

Books produced by Time-Life Custom Publishing are available at special bulk discount for promotional and premium use. Custom adaptations can also be created to meet your specific marketing goals.

Call 1-800-323-5255

Library of Congress Cataloging in Publication Data

Fields, Debbi.
    Mrs. Fields best cookie book ever! : 130 delicious cookie and dessert recipes from the kitchen of Mrs. Fields / by Debbi Fields and the editors of Time-Life Books.
        p.   cm. --
    Includes index.
    ISBN 0-7835-4830-3 (softcover) 0-7835-4910-5 (hardcover)
    1. Cookies. 2. Desserts. I. Time-Life Books. II. Title.
TX772.F53 1996
641.8'654 - - dc20   96-19360
                                                            CIP